# JURY TRIALS: THE PSYCHOLOGY OF WINNING STRATEGY

**DONALD E. VINSON**

THE MICHIE COMPANY
Law Publishers
Charlottesville, Virginia

---

Library of Congress Card Number 86-62258
ISBN 0-87215-993-0

---

**For Katie and Mark**
**whose father**
**spends entirely too much**
**time in courtrooms,**
**lawyers' offices and airports**

# TABLE OF CONTENTS

# FOREWORD

This book was written for trial lawyers — those people who are, in actuality, the real psychologists who deal with human behavior in courtrooms every day throughout the country. For those people whose daily lives involve the use and application of behavioral science in the courtroom but who may lack formal training, this book will: (1) provide a number of contemporary perspectives and specific recommendations for the use of behavioral strategies in the courtroom; and (2) offer explanations as to why certain strategies and tactics employed by successful trial lawyers are effective.

I am indebted to many superb trial lawyers who have provided me with the insights and experiences upon which behavioral theory and practical application have come together. To date, my firm, Litigation Sciences, has been involved in more than 700 cases utilizing many of the tools and techniques discussed in this book. Based on these experiences, I have attempted to make the book relevant for lawyers who go to court. However, *Jury Trials: The Psychology of Winning Strategy* was not designed to be a definitive compendium or handbook of social science theory applied to the law. Rather, it was written to provide busy people with an overview of the topic which will hopefully be interesting, provocative, and enjoyable to read.

In addition to the influence of clients and friends, I would also like to thank my colleagues at Litigation Sciences for their helpful comments and input to this book. In particular, I am grateful for the counsel and advice of Steve Van Voorhis in our New York office, Farrald Belote in Houston, Robert Wiss and Philip Anthony in Los Angeles, and Steven Holder in London. Finally, I would like to acknowledge the superb typing and editorial assistance Betty Peer provided during the course of this project.

*Donald E. Vinson*

Los Angeles, 1986

# INTRODUCTION

*Jury Trials: The Psychology of Winning Strategy* is based upon the application of social science theories and techniques to more than 700 cases. From the experience of helping attorneys develop winning results in these trial proceedings, a number of important general strategic perspectives have emerged concerning juries and how they work. We have learned that there are key moments and key issues in every trial. The prediction and control of the trial process rests upon taking advantage of these key moments and issues.

The strategic perspectives developed in this book have been formulated through consultation with many different clients throughout the United States. Cases involved include product liability, antitrust, securities, intellectual property, wrongful discharge, and contract litigation, among others. Yet the concepts presented in this book are not specific to any particular type of lawsuit. For the most part, they are of general application. Their successful implementation, however, depends upon highly specific pretrial preparation in each individual case.

This is a book on the general subject of psychological strategy. This means that its content consists of a number of topics based on broad areas of concern. It has been said that there are key moments in every trial. These are voir dire, the opening statement, the presentation of certain critical visual communications, and the testimony of key witnesses. Critical issues for jurors in any trial are relatively small numbers of anchoring ideas which they use to form their own understanding of a case. These ideas can be legal points, but they are often psychological or emotional issues which may not be immediately evident from a legal standpoint. An important part of psychological strategy in any trial is aimed at uncovering these key issues.

Bearing in mind, then, a general approach to the trial grounded on the notion of key moments and key issues, the social sciences offer a number of important theoretical orientations. These theoretical orientations are proven theories about how people behave which can be applied to the courtroom. Jurors are not extraordinary. They meet expected norms of human behavior. Knowledge of the general manner in which people act and solve problems in daily life is the starting point for forming psychological trial strategy.

It is important to note, then, that this book is not a compendium of specific strategies or trial tips for attorneys. It might be possible to write a book entitled *101 Ways to Influence a Jury,* or *Rules for the Psychological Conduct of Voir Dire,* but this is not such a book. Such books are likely to purchase neatness at the expense of oversimplification. They are more likely to promise more than they can deliver. There are instances in this book when highly specific strategies are noted. Occasionally there will be do's and do not's for attorneys to consider, but overall the point of this book is to present areas in which psychological strategy is important and necessary and to show that certain leading ideas held by social psychologists can be used by attorneys as a framework within which to formulate general and specific approaches to any given trial.

This can be illustrated with a few simple observations. It is very important for attorneys, for example, to try to discover something about a juror's verdict preference in voir dire, or even prior to voir dire. Psychologists have shown that people decide between alternative explanations of someone else's behavior by using attitudes already in place. These attitudes concern the behavior under evaluation and the person being judged. This psychological insight about the importance of prior attitudes is the basis for trial strategy in general and for specific strategic and tactical approaches in each individual case.

A second example concerns memory and retention. Communications psychologists have established that people tend to remember the information they hear first longer than information that comes later. This gives rise to the general proposition, long confirmed by many findings, that jurors tend to retain information which is presented at the beginning and at the end much better than other information they receive during the middle of the trial.

The ability to form trial strategies based on such psychological principles gives attorneys a powerful tool. The framework of legal issues upon which any case is adjudicated is certainly critical and must remain primary. But beyond that, jurors invariably find many other aspects of human behavior and character relevant. Through the institution of the jury, American jurisprudence insures that issues of human behavior and psychology will be germane in any court of law. Legal strategies, then, can be supplemented by those which are purely behavioral or psychological in nature.

## The Plan Of This Book

In keeping with the suggestion that trial psychological strategies need to be built around key moments and key issues in a trial, the chapter content of this book is based on such moments and issues. Juror attitudes and the way in which they will be mobilized in a given trial make up the basis for a number of important strategic orientations. These attitudes are the central issue in formulating what can be called content strategy. What should the basic content of the case presentation be? From a behavioral standpoint, it should center on the issues jurors will find most salient. These issues can be discovered in pretrial research using groups of surrogate jurors and verified in large scale juror attitude surveys.

Juror attitudes and opinions, in the form of beliefs, values, and sometimes prejudice and bias, are the framework jurors use to interpret the facts of a case. These attitudes, opinions, values, and beliefs are also used to attribute blame by jurors. This subject is discussed at length in Chapter 1.

Our approach to the key moments of the trial, such as voir dire, opening statement, key witness testimony, and the presentation of important visual exhibits is to consider these moments primarily as problems in communication. As problems in communication, understanding these key moments will also require the integration of our research on attitudes and attributions into an overall communications approach. In other words, we can form strategy using psychological principles of effective communication but must continue to refer back to what we know about juror attitudes and attributions in determining the basic content of the messages we send.

Strategies, then, which govern the use of visual exhibits or communications, use the psychological principles of perception. These are discussed in Chapter 2. In Chapter 3, strategies which involve how jurors apportion blame will be the principle topic. Jurors apportion blame by employing a process called attribution, an important area of research for social psychologists. Chapter 4 identifies the problem of juror bias from a psychological perspective and examines bias in the context of examples from three high profile cases. In Chapter 5, the specific problems of attorney and witness credibility, considered as a matter of communication strategy, make up the content. The voir dire process is examined in Chapter 6, and a new alternative approach to the traditional practice of evaluating jurors is presented. Chapter 7 focuses on the fundamental matter of juror selection and reviews the role of juror profiles in making informed selection decisions. Chapter 8 concentrates on another key moment in the trial, the opening statement, and lays out some basic strategic perspectives for the organization and delivery of opening statements. Finally, in Chapter 9, we will review a number of the more important conceptual and methodological techniques available to assist trial lawyers implement social science strategies in litigation.

Psychological trial strategies do not offer attorneys magic formulas for winning cases. These strategies are based on painstaking pretrial preparations which fundamentally consist of empirical research on scientific principles. There are intuitive, if not artistic, elements in developing strategy of this kind, and its success is dependent upon the skill of the practitioners, both with regard to its formulation and its use.

Attorneys can learn to use behavioral strategies if they are willing to approach the subject with open minds and to blend their legal orientation with a behavioral one. It is hoped that this book will further these efforts.

CHAPTER 1

# JUROR ATTITUDES: THE BASIC STRATEGIC CONSIDERATION



Consistent with what many trial lawyers suspect, jurors do not typically come to conclusions by an inductive process of carefully weighing and sifting evidence. Inductive thinking is thinking which begins with the collection and interpretation of specific information and then forming opinions and conclusions. It is a mental calculation in which the sum of factual information yields general conclusions. In a jury context, inductive thinking represents the balancing of evidence for first one side and then the other and then making inferences and verdict decisions.

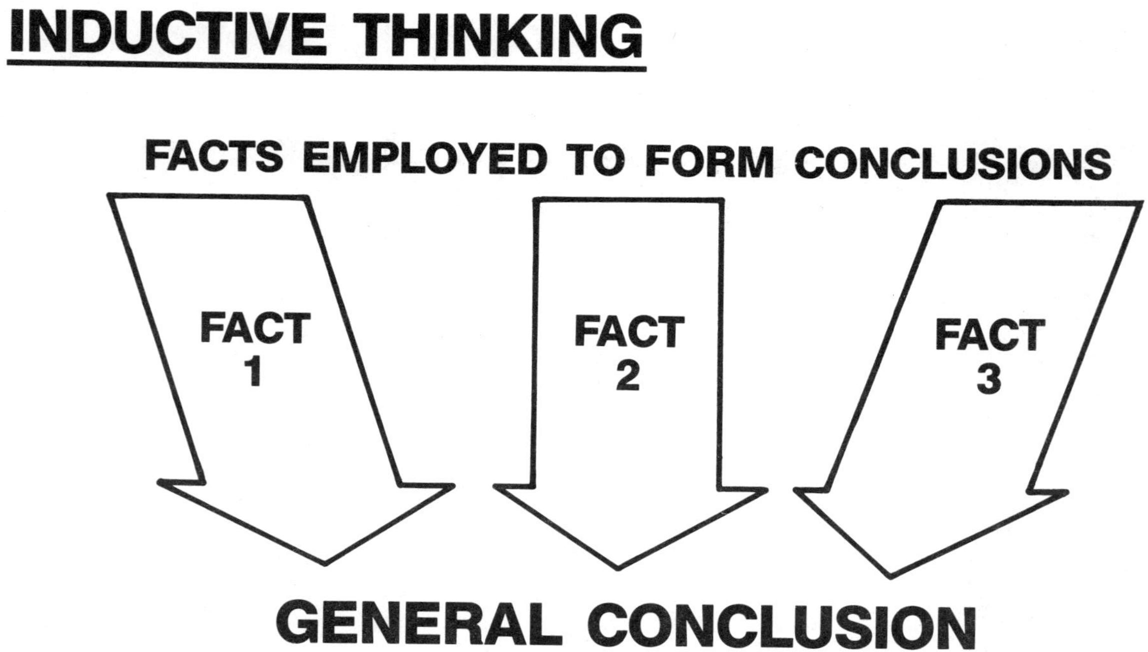
INDUCTIVE THINKING
FACTS EMPLOYED TO FORM CONCLUSIONS
FACT 1
FACT 2
FACT 3
GENERAL CONCLUSION

FIGURE 1

Many people, however, do not reach conclusions inductively. They make immediate judgments and then seek support for their view from available information. Most jurors, for example, typically reason deductively. They latch onto a few fundamental premises and fit the facts to these premises as they are received. Philosophers call deductive thinking reasoning from the general to the particular.

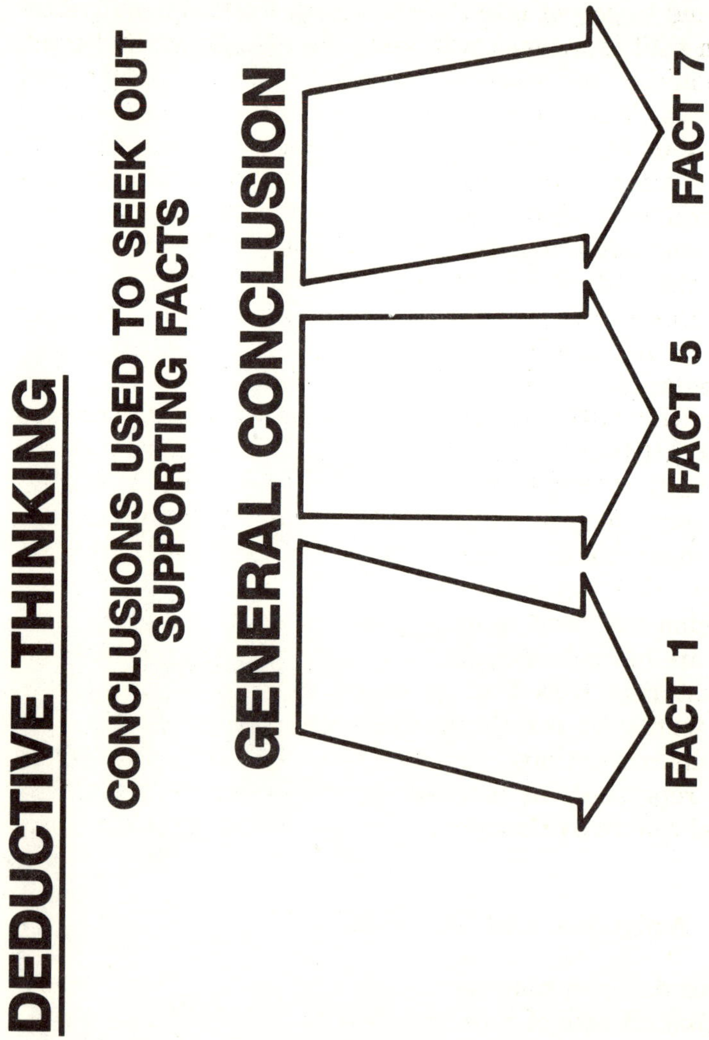
DEDUCTIVE THINKING
CONCLUSIONS USED TO SEEK OUT SUPPORTING FACTS
GENERAL CONCLUSION
FACT 1
FACT 5
FACT 7

FIGURE 2

The ideas or premises jurors bring with them into the courtroom constitute what psychologists call cognitive structures. Cognitions pertain to what we know. Cognitive structures are made up of what we *think* we know. While cognitive structures enable us to learn things that are new, they tend to perpetuate themselves by screening out information that is inconsistent with what is already believed. Occasionally, we encounter people who are flexible and "objective," but this is frequently the result of some special training or higher education. Such people do, on occasion, become jurors. For the most part, however, lawyers encounter a great deal of cognitive inflexibility among jurors. Their cognitive structures act as a mechanism through which they admit information consistent with what is already there. Hence, most jurors strive to reach verdicts which do not conflict strongly with cognitions in place at the beginning of the trial.

Cognitions are frequently associated with such words as beliefs, attitudes, opinions, or values. They can often be inferred from what an individual says or does. However, these cognitions differ in several important respects. The most important differences relate to their duration and intensity. Our opinions are usually related to current questions and tend to be temporary. Our beliefs and attitudes are more deep-seated and lasting. Although no hard-and-fast rule says that we must describe differences in these terms, we can think of opinions as impressions, attitudes as convictions, and beliefs as values. Because attitudes represent an individual's convictions, they play a central role in evaluating alternatives and in making decisions.

## § 1-1. Attitudes and Decisions.

Juror decision making is a specific act of human behavior. Like all acts of human behavior, it is based on a complex fabric of informational inputs. Behavioral researchers have attempted to understand what kinds of jurors reach what types of decisions and how attitudes affect the way in which jurors must be informed and persuaded toward a particular view in a trial. Jurors do not come into the courtroom with a blank slate or *tabula rasa.* They bring with them a large number of attitudes which are firmly entrenched in their minds. Many psychologists believe that by an early age people possess an inventory of strongly held attitudes and beliefs which are used to make judgments and evaluations throughout the rest of their lives. In fact, the way we make decisions is by juxtaposing information against these attitudes. In coming to conclusions and in making judgments or decisions, we use what we believe to be true as a template for evaluating new information. In this manner, our attitudes act as a kind of filter or screen. Jurors themselves may not recognize that they possess certain beliefs which may hinder their fair assessment of new information even though these stop short of explicit prejudice toward one of the litigants. No one, in this sense, is ever intellectually neutral.

In an antitrust case, a large corporation was accused of having created a monopoly. Plaintiff claimed that the corporation had unfairly dominated technology and prevented competition through several practices alleged to be in violation of antitrust laws. The defendant was accused of announcing new products prior to reasonable schedules of availability. The corporation was also alleged to have deliberately redesigned products to make them incompatible with replacement units supplied by the plaintiff. These, and related allegations, did not figure, however, in the jurors' verdict in favor of the defendant. The overriding attitude which governed the jurors' decision was that the defendant corporation deserved to reap the benefits of its enterprise and technological superiority. Plaintiff's claims were found to be only of minimal importance.

## § 1-2. What Are Attitudes?

Pretrial research into juror attitudes is the most important strategic application of social science to the law. Research into juror attitudes has two main objectives. By learning what attitudes jurors will use in deciding a case, we will have an important tool at our disposal in juror selection. At the same time, we will have gained insight into the salient issues that will form the foundation of a jury's verdict.

Psychologists define an attitude as a disposition to like or dislike some object or person. There is little in life that we regard with absolute neutrality. We have attitudes toward just about everything. These attitudes are often learned from our parents and peers. They are often the result of a positive or negative experience. Sometimes they develop through observing the behavior of others. Most of us like to think our attitudes are rational, consistent, and based on the truth. And we generally hold a number of basic beliefs about life with which we expect our attitudes to be consistent. We may believe that people are basically honest. Our attitudes will reflect this belief. We may believe that big business is basically duplicitous. Our attitudes will reflect this belief. We may believe that riding a motorcycle is dangerous. Our attitudes will be consistent with this.

Attitudes result from a person's value system, and the development of this value system begins as a child. Our values are modified as a result of learning and experiences. We can determine a person's values to some extent by observing his social background, education, occupation, and chronologic stage of life. The attitudes that people hold determine their interest patterns and are reflected in their actions.

The term attitude can be used to connote how an individual thinks or feels about something. From a cognitive point of view, an attitude represents an organization of balanced cognitions: the things people know — the things they believe. From a motivational point of view, an attitude represents a state of readiness for motive arousal. For our purposes, attitudes are preferences or inclinations to act toward some specific objects, events, or situations. They are comprised of cognitive, affective, and conative processes that tend to interact with one another and reinforce the attitude. The cognitive component of an attitude relates to what people think. The affective component defines what they feel. The conative portion of an attitude represents the behavioral or manifest component. Thus, all attitudes contain an intellectual, higher order belief aspect as well as a feeling or emotional element. To challenge or reinforce an attitude, then, the trial lawyer must understand which component of the attitude he is attempting to influence.

In a litigation environment, the psychologist's interest in attitudes stems from the desire to predict juror behavior on the basis of these intervening and measurable variables. If jurors are favorably inclined toward the plaintiff or defendant, the attorney may wish to institute communications designed to maintain and reinforce this favorable attitude. On the other hand, if jurors view one of the parties unfavorably, attitude change procedures may be necessary. In situations where jurors are unfamiliar with a party to the litigation or with major issues which are salient to the case, the attorney is faced with the task of creating *new* attitudes which are favorable to his client. Thus we can see in the course of attempts at persuasion, the lawyers may seek to: (1) *confirm* existing attitudes; (2) *change* existing attitudes; or (3) *create* new attitudes.

## § 1-3. Attitude Sets.

An attitude generally does not exist in isolation from other attitudes. Attitude components tend to be consistent and correspond to other attitudes within attitude sets. For example, a juror's attitudes about sports may tend to relate to attitudes about entertainment or relaxation. Thus, attitudes as a whole tend to form clusters with other attitudes within a person's total attitudinal system. Although complete harmony need not exist, it would be expected that attitudes making up cognitive structure would be fairly consistent. Thus, for example, an individual is not likely to accept the findings of the Surgeon General's report concerning cigarette smoking and believe at the same time that cigarette smoking is harmless. Hence, it would be expected that attitudes comprising an attitude cluster or set would tend towards consistency, although this is not always the case. If a juror is a staunch Republican and possesses probusiness attitudes, he would not be expected to vote for the award of large punitive damages unless, of course, other attitudinal clusters were more relevant. These might include his attitudes toward corporate responsibility or competition in the marketplace.

Juror attitudes do not come into play in a trial randomly. Trial content and the issues involved will mobilize juror attitudes in clusters or constellations. These constellations or attitude sets are related to specific trial content. Often there will be aspects of the trial with which jurors have had previous experience. In product liability cases, they may have used similar products. In securities litigation, they may have made or lost money investing in the stock market. Attitude sets which grow out of these experiences are behaviorally based attitudes.

Attitudes can also form clusters in accord with demographic factors. A person's level of education, age, income, sex, or religious and political preferences can all partially determine what attitudes they will hold.

Research findings based on relationships between specific political attitudes and verdict have been reported for jurors who favor capital punishment and severe sentences. Jurors who favor capital punishment are more likely to vote for conviction in a murder trial, and jurors with positive attitudes toward law and order favor severe sentences. Attitudes toward the crime itself are also probably important determinants of a verdict. Jurors who do not favor particular statutes, like those which pertain to victimless crimes, for example, will show a tendency to favor the defendant. Attitudes toward the specific circumstances of the crime can also be significant in certain instances. Bias in rape cases is commonplace because of attitudes toward the circumstances of the crime, the physical location, the kind of clothing worn by the victim, the time of day, and so forth. It is also probably true that with the rise of feminist consciousness and a general change in how male-female relationships are viewed, attitudes toward rape as a serious crime have changed as well. Data suggests that over the decade 1970-1980, rapists were judged more harshly as time went on.

## § 1-4. Attitude Formation.

While attitudes are developed in a number of ways, most psychologists believe that they are learned by a process of information acquisition and through social interaction. Factors affecting attitude formation and change are numerous, but most authorities on the subject believe that the most important of these can be summarized as follows:

*Biological Motivation.* It is inevitable that some attitudes are formed as the individual attempts to satisfy his most basic drives and needs. Through this process, people tend to develop favorable attitudes toward other people, objects and events which satisfy their needs and develop unfavorable attitudes toward those which block the attainment of satisfaction or drive reduction.

*Information.* Attitudes are based to some extent upon the nature and amount of information an individual receives and upon the nature of its source. Attorneys generally view information as a significant influence in achieving attitude change on the part of jurors, but selective perception explains why there is not a perfect relationship between the information a person receives and what he incorporates into his belief system. Nevertheless, information is indeed *one* of the sources for achieving the formation of new attitudes or changes in old ones.

*Group Affiliations.* Many of the attitudes held by jurors come either directly or indirectly from primary or membership groups. Sociologists refer to these groups as consisting of significant others and include family, church, work, and social relationships. These groups are important not only in the values which they hold but also in the amount and type of information that they transmit to an individual. In this respect, group affiliations are important as a major force in determining attitude development.

*Personality.* There are aspects of an individual's personality which impact on the development of attitudes and affect the process of attitude change. These include dominance, sociability, responsibility, compliance, and activity levels to name only a few.

*Experience.* Actual experience with an object, event, or person has enormous influence on a person's predispositions toward a specific attitude object. In a jury context, a negative experience with a litigant's product or service might produce a negative reaction strong enough to affect the individual's ultimate evaluation of that party in the litigation.

## § 1-5. Attitude Change.

It is possible to infer from what has been said so far that attitudes and beliefs are rigid and immutable. This is not entirely so. One course of action open to jurors who suffer the collision of new information with basic attitudes is to change these attitudes. Attitude change is a change from a disposition to act in one direction to a disposition to act in the opposite direction (from disliking to liking an object, person or event). Often, without meaning to, lawyers find themselves asking jurors to do this. The attorney's world of logical argument involves the construction of an unshakable edifice of proof based upon the careful piling-up of fact upon fact. While such an approach may be effective in attitude change with some jurors, it is not likely to work with the vast majority of people who serve on juries. In order to change attitudes, attorneys must carry out a direct emotional assault on the attitudes or beliefs in question.

Most attempts to affect change in juror attitudes rely upon persuasive information, and the cognitive component of the attitude is the most frequent target of attitude change. Attorneys rely upon the communication of information to bring about changes in beliefs which will hopefully lead to changes in attitude. Although this is the most logical means of attitude change open to the attorney, its relative success is not particularly great.

Some psychologists have suggested that the alteration of the affective or *feeling* component of an attitude can bring about alterations in the cognitive component. For an example, a plaintiff attorney may seek to create a "mood" with his opening statement or through the use of his witnesses to produce feelings of sadness or fear in a products liability case. If the jury accepts this mood, changes in both components of attitudes may result. It is interesting to note that a considerable amount of consumer advertising operates on the creation of moods or feelings to impact upon the affective component of attitudes toward commercial products rather than on the cognitive component.

Attitudes are closely linked to the way we behave. In fact, there is evidence that we form attitudes in part by observing our own behavior and drawing the appropriate conclusions. The product choices we make as consumers are a form of behavior that is often the basis for attitudes and attitude shifts. A man may have purchased a succession of large American cars over the years. During this period he probably expressed the following attitudes: "I like large cars because they are safer and more comfortable than little cars. I like the way large cars look, long, and streamlined, as opposed to looking like little cans or boxes on wheels. I don't like small foreign cars. They are made for smaller people, for congested Asian cities, they are underpowered, and so forth." For reasons of economy, among others, this man may decide to purchase a small, compact car of foreign make. With this new behavior, there will be an accompanying attitude shift. Formerly held positive attitudes toward large cars will become muted, and in its place will emerge a new set of more positive attitudes toward small cars.

As we have said, individuals are almost always more resistant to attitude change than to attitude reinforcement. For this reason, it may be easier for the attorney to introduce a new idea or concept toward a significant aspect of his case and attempt to engage in attitude creation than try to change an existing unfavorable attitude.

## § 1-6. Attitude Salience.

Jurors hold thousands of attitudes. Some are highly salient, important, and centrally held while others are of less significance. Salience refers to the strength with which attitudes are held. Salience tends to be situation specific, however. An attitude can be very strongly held in one psychological context and of less significance in another. For example, a juror's attitude toward the safety features of a particular automobile may be less salient in a purchase situation than say, attitudes towards styling, speed, prestige, or economy. However, if the same individual were a juror evaluating the same automobile in a products liability case in which a small child was seriously injured, attitudes toward the product's safety may now become significantly more salient. Hence, while it is important for trial lawyers to understand the attitudes that jurors are likely to bring with them into the courtroom, it is *critical* that they understand the salience of attitudes which are likely to be associated with issues or factors in their case.

The only way to really understand what attitudes jurors hold and the salience of these attitudes is to undertake carefully designed pretrial research studies. When properly conducted, these studies focus on what kinds of jurors hold which attitudes, the structural composition of these attitudes, and the salience with which they are held.

In a major antitrust case in which Litigation Sciences was involved, jurors were questioned by the judge during voir dire as to their attitudes toward the defendant in the case. Not surprisingly and indeed totally consistent with our pretrial research, almost every juror expressed negative opinions toward the defendant and its level of service in the community. While these responses may have otherwise provided the trial attorneys with a great deal of discomfort, pretrial research had revealed that these attitudes, while widely held, would not be salient in the specific context of this case. Rather, attitudes toward technology, innovation, and scientific expertise were more determinant and correlated with verdict preference. Hence, the strategy in this particular case was designed to focus on those attitudes which were positively associated with the defendant rather than attempting to change negative ones without high salience or importance.

## § 1-7. Attitudes and Behavior.

Sometimes jurors appear to distort and twist evidence until it becomes consistent with their attitudes. In an employment discrimination case, videotape depositions were viewed by male and female jurors. In post-trial interviews, women jurors recalled seeing the depositions of the female plaintiff presented in a black and white videotape by the defense. These same women jurors recalled seeing the depositions of men in color. These women then concluded that the defense had engaged in a ploy by presenting women's depositions in black and white and those by men in color. This ploy was seen as an attempt to influence the jurors against the female defendant. In fact, all the depositions shown by the defense were in color. Female jurors had engaged in selective perception.

With carefully designed research efforts, it is often possible to come up with accurate predictions of a person's attitude based on the way he behaves. This was done in a case involving soft drink bottlers in which we identified attitudinal and behavioral constellations which were predictors of verdict preference.

### Case Study: The Soft Drink Bottlers

Litigation Sciences became involved in a case involving soft drink bottlers. It was very important to establish juror profiles on the basis of attitudes. These profiles could then be used in voir dire and also as a basis for determining Psychological Anchors.

In this instance, an independent bottler alleged that a large bottler/distributor with a competing brand had utilized its trademarks and brand names to monopolize shelf space at the retail level. Our initial simulated trial research had shown that the facts in the case were sufficient to elicit strong opinions on the part of both plaintiff and defendant jurors.

We worked for the defendant and undertook a major research effort aimed at identifying reactions to case issues and the development of juror types who would be favorably or unfavorably predisposed to the client. After extensive small group issue identification studies, a large scale juror attitude survey was undertaken.

The survey design incorporated two kinds of questions: a list of proposed voir dire questions and questions which came out of our analysis of the qualitative or small group research. This small group work had indicated that in addition to demographic questions, three general attitudinal and experiential areas should be explored in the survey. These were:

1. General consumer attitudes toward soft drink products, brand loyalty, and soft drink consumption habits.
2. Knowledge of and feelings about monopoly, restraint of trade, antitrust laws, and competition.
3. Attitudes involving perceptions of business conduct, businessmen, and "fair play."

While profiles of plaintiff and defendant jurors based on demographic variables like sex, income, age, education, religion, and political preference are deemed desirable because they are readily observable measures, we have found that attitudinal and personality variables are often better predictors of a juror's behavior. Sometimes demographic and attitudinal variables can be correlated. This yields most useful information for voir dire. We then know what kind of people are likely to have what kind of attitudes.

In responses to our survey, prospective jurors told us whether or not they favored the defendant or plaintiff. We then sought to link these verdict preferences with answers to other survey question items. While no one answer predicted verdict preference reliably by itself, it was found that constellations of answers would do so. Each of these constellations, clusters, or patterns was based on responses to three or more questions.

## § 1-8. Attitude Constellations.

The first constellation was related to health concerns regarding soft drinks. Among survey respondents, there was a small, but identifiable group who expressed concern about the health hazards posed by the sugar and/or chemical content of soft drinks. These people significantly limited their intake and their children's intake of soft drinks.

Jurors found in this first constellation proved to be ideal for the defense. When they did purchase or consume soft drinks, they exhibited a high degree of trust in brand names. They saw brand name products as less dangerous and more desirable than secondary brands or private label products. They believed it was worthwhile to purchase a premium product even though it was purchased infrequently. They equated the defendant's brand name with such a premium, and hence, safe product.

For the group of people included in this first constellation, another set of attitudes was linked to the attitudinal/behavioral cluster represented by product use and purchase pattern. These people tended to be skeptical of allegations of monopoly. Consistent with these attitudes, they aggressively sought out reasons to discount the claims of the plaintiff.

It was also possible to match demographic correlates to this first constellation. With the exception of some older women with an educational level exceeding high school, people in this first constellation tended to fall within a range of 30 to 45 years of age.

The second attitude constellation we identified as a predictor of verdict preference was strictly behavioral in nature. It was related to soft drink preference and habits of consumption. Furthermore, this constellation was made up of three subgroups. These were:

1. Heavy consumers of soft drinks who were brand loyal.
2. Heavy consumers of soft drinks who were not brand loyal.
3. Those who virtually never consumed soft drinks but purchased soft drinks regularly for entertaining.

Although these people all had a number of attitudes in common, their actual behavior and their specific attitudes toward the trial varied.

The last group, subgroup 3, proved most strongly anti-defendant. Like the health concerned people in the first constellation, they purchased only name brands. Their brand loyalty, however, was motivated by caution and a lack of inclination to take social risks, not by taste preferences. When these people were exposed to the claims of the plaintiff, they felt manipulated by soft drink producers and became antagonistic to certain marketing and advertising practices of brand name bottlers. When provided with an opportunity to render a decision in this case, there was almost universal agreement with plaintiff's position. While small in number, the members of this group were more articulate in supporting their verdict than the others; hence, they were judged to be especially dangerous to the defense.

On the surface of things, subgroup 2, those who consumed heavily but were not brand loyal, might be taken as the most dangerous to the defendant. Not so. The opposite proved to be the case. Apparently, plaintiff's allegations did not comport with their everyday experience of being able to readily purchase a variety of different brands.

As predicted, subgroup 1, the brand loyal heavy consumers, were favorable to the defense. They attributed their brand loyalty to taste differences and discounted plaintiff's assertions as a trivial excuse to justify poor sales for inferior brands.

The third attitude constellation which proved useful in the construction of juror profiles in this case was unrelated to soft drinks *per se.* Instead, it tapped an individual's preexisting beliefs about the dynamics of small and large businesses. The people here who proved to be the strongest advocates for the plaintiff were not hostile toward big business. But they tended to be intensely committed to the virtues of small business in American society. Simple, straightforward inquiries into attitudes toward monopoly, or monopoly power, during voir dire would most likely fail to identify these particular juror types.

Once the attitudinal and behavioral constellations for favorable and unfavorable jurors had been discovered, it was possible to devise a paradigm for scoring prospective jurors on each constellation or dimension based on their answers to voir dire questions. Obviously, it is not always possible to score people on every dimension. Data will be incomplete, or there will be inconsistent responses within a particular content area. In this case, the constellations were largely independent of each other. This meant that a prospective juror who scored within the unfavorable range on *any* of the three constellations was considered a candidate for a peremptory challenge.

Thus, by applying the concept of attitudes and attitude constellations in pretrial research, it was possible to prepare ourselves adequately for voir dire.

## § 1-9. Conclusions.

As we have seen, jurors may not follow the web of inference into which attorneys seek to draw them. In fact, jurors, because they are people, frequently do not attend to the vast majority of "information" presented in the courtroom. Indeed, they cannot. Unlike computers, human beings have a limited capacity to perceive, interpret, and store information. Post-trial interviews consistently reveal that jurors tend to forget a large number of details in any trial. For example, key witnesses are sometimes forgotten or misidentified. Telling pieces of demonstrative evidence, often obtained at great expense, may be simply forgotten. While frustrating, these are facts that trial lawyers have to contend with when developing strategies designed to influence the jury decision-making process.

Juror decision making is a psychological process in which a juror's own basic attitudes and beliefs are blended with an attorney's theory of the case. Hence, the need to identify attitudes and attitudinal configurations is a basic strategic consideration in any trial. It begins with the premise that people enter the courtroom with an array of attitudes and beliefs already in place which are based on previous experience and knowledge. Jurors are frequently in a stressful position, and new information which is not consistent with these attitudes will only increase their discomfort. As a result, they may engage in a variety of coping behaviors to avoid changing existing beliefs. They may distort evidence, and they will frequently overlook evidence altogether. Always, the information they receive will be interpreted in ways which are consistent with what jurors want or need to believe.

The first step in using knowledge about attitudes as a trial strategy is to learn what kind of people are going to be on the jury. To do so it is necessary to use personal interviews and juror attitude surveys. These surveys frequently come from the close study of surrogate jurors evaluating the case in small groups. The identification of attitudinal structures emerges from statistical and qualitative analysis and is carefully tested and refined before being implemented in the courtroom. An overview of the basic research tools and techniques appropriate for juror attitude research will be presented in Chapter 9.

# CHAPTER 2

# HOW JURORS SEE AND HEAR: THE IMPORTANCE OF PERCEPTUAL STRATEGY



In this chapter, we will focus on perceptual problems jurors have in the courtroom and offer a number of strategies for dealing with these problems. In Chapter 1, it was seen how previously held attitudes and beliefs could cause jurors to deal with evidence in particular ways. As we saw, there was an unconscious motivation behind this process brought about by the need to maintain psychological consistency. Another aspect of how jurors perceive and remember evidence involves the sense organs *per se*. There are many occasions when the eyes and ears of jurors simply fail to operate the way an attorney would like. The psychology of sense perception is a well-developed field from which we can glean a great deal of useful information about the perceptual problems of jurors.

## § 2-1. Psychology of Sense Perception.

The psychology of sense perception is one of the oldest and most developed of the social sciences. Many laboratory experiments have been conducted in the area of sense perception, and a large body of evidence has accumulated. The data from these experiments illustrate many principles of human perception. They tell us how our senses work, and when and why they fail to work.

Our knowledge of sense perception and how it functions has been applied in a variety of practical ways. Graphic designers, advertising artists, and media experts have all employed the principles of sensory perception in their work. These principles play a major part in the marketing of goods and are used by most professional communicators, from broadcast journalists to script writers. Recently, they have begun to be applied to the law.

In the simplest of terms, perception can be described as the process of becoming aware of our world directly through any of the senses. It also means becoming aware in one's mind — to understand and apprehend. Perception can be said to mean the overall process which includes the activity of the person that accompanies or immediately follows the awareness acquired through the senses. It is the entire process by which an individual becomes aware of his environment and interprets it so that it will fit into his own frame of reference. Thus, every courtroom perception (jurors of lawyers as well as lawyers of jurors) involves some person who becomes aware, through the senses, of some thing, act, or event.

The perception of jurors concerns how the individual views himself and the events that occur in the courtroom. Individuals are different, in part, because they perceive differently.

Perception is selective because individual minds fail to comprehend and interpret all the sensations that bombard the senses at any given time. Human beings can attend to only a limited amount of available stimuli or information. Three mechanisms exist in the perceptual process that govern which stimuli will "get through" to the mind and which will not. These are perceptual overloading, selective sensitization, and perceptual defense.

Perceptual overloading occurs because at any given time jurors can take in and bring up to a conscious level only relatively few of the stimuli confronting them. The individual finds it impossible to respond to everything at once. Through perception, a juror is able to select from among the stimuli. In this manner, an individual makes his decisions manageable. The selective nature of perception is a result of the subjective nature of people and of the limited capacity of human sensory equipment. Selective sensitization occurs when individuals perceive stimuli both accurately and rapidly because these stimuli are congruous with their value orientation. Perceptual defense occurs when a person's value orientation not only contributes to his selection of stimuli but also acts to erect barriers to those stimuli seen as threats. Thus, people are more than normally perceptive to some sensations and less than normally perceptive to others. The result is a type of natural perceptual bias that exists in all situations. This includes the courtroom.

The selectiveness of perception brought about by the physiological inability to take in more than a few stimuli at one time has importance to litigators. There are limits to the human capacity to absorb messages accurately. A lawyer's argument is thus competing with many other available information inputs, even though only a small percentage of these are seen and brought to a conscious level by the juror. Selective perception dictates not only carefully planned issue selection but also the number of elements presented in the case and how they are presented.

## § 2-2. Juror Perceptual Tendencies.

People use their senses to maintain contact with the external world. A constant stream of stimuli emanates from this world, and from this stream of stimuli we use our sense organs to gather information. Out of all the impressions that come at us, we process a relatively small number.

Jurors are constantly bombarded with more perceptual data than they can process. Characteristically, they screen out a great many of these perceptions. They selectively pick out details which are consistent with their attitudes and preconceptions and organize what they see and hear into messages. The organization of this information may or may not represent the message intended by the sender of the information. Like anyone else, to a large extent jurors see what they want to see, hear what they want to hear, and perceive what they want to perceive. The patterns of juror perceptions are consistent with their past experience and with what they think ought to be. Most jurors perceive the world in ways which are consistent with their attitudes, values, and beliefs.

In a negligence case, a great deal of scientific and technical data was presented to show that bacteria had been introduced into a patient's body through the implementation of an artificial heart valve. The patient had died from a massive pulmonary infection. Plaintiffs alleged medical malpractice. The defense claimed that an existing infection simply attached itself to the device after it had been implanted. Expert testimony tended to indicate that the valve had not been sterilized properly and that it had been carelessly inserted.

Jurors were interviewed after the trial, and it was discovered that they attached little weight to plaintiff's expert testimony. They believed that the level of general competence in the medical community was high enough to insure that the valve had been properly sterilized. They also believed that standards of quality control in the medical products industry were so high that a defective valve could not have been manufactured. Thus, attitudes which they had in place at the start of the trial clashed directly with expert testimony. As is usually the case, previously held attitudes held sway.

From this, it is obvious that jurors perceive many things that occur during a trial according to pre-existing cognitions. These values, attitudes, and beliefs result in the kind of memory tricks and distorted perception we have just been discussing. It should be stressed that this is an unconscious process and can be done without malice by well-meaning and very conscientious jurors. Nevertheless, it is an important factor which must be taken into consideration in the planning of all juror strategy.

Another reason why jurors pay attention selectively in the courtroom is due to the fact that they may be in a position of relatively high psychological stress. They are unfamiliar with courtroom customs and procedures. They are strangers in an environment in which the judge and attorneys are at home. Furthermore, they initially lack the overall comprehension of the case possessed by the other courtroom players, particularly attorneys, who have just undergone laborious preparations for trial. They use their cognitions and selective attention to begin to "cut matters down to size."

## § 2-2(A). Person Perception.

Are jurors affected by their perceptions of other people in the courtroom? Studies have confirmed that jurors do react to the perceived character and appearance of the defendant in criminal cases. Unattractive defendants are judged more harshly than attractive ones and are sentenced to longer terms of incarceration. In general, punitive tendencies are decreased in a way that is directly proportional to the defendant's attractiveness. However, the attractiveness of the defendant does not mitigate the sentence when the defendant's physical appearance was a necessary component in the crime. In studies where a male swindler took advantage of women, in part because of his charm and good looks, the advantage that would otherwise accrue to a physically attractive defendant was nullified.

In addition to physical appearance, jurors have revealed in post-trial interviews that attire has influenced their perception of courtroom participants. In a major case involving a contract dispute between two large corporations, jurors discounted the testimony of the chairman of the board of one of the companies. When interviewed after the trial, jurors were in agreement that this man could not be taken seriously. A person of his supposed stature and prominence would have known not to wear loafer shoes with a three-piece suit. Sound silly? All of us make attributions and form perceptions of other people on attire, language, accent, and grooming on a daily basis. In fact, there have been a number of popular books written to advise young lawyers and aspiring businessmen on how to dress for success, order wine with authority, and vacation with sophistication. While it may seem like a mundane detail, trial lawyers should very carefully monitor the perceptual impressions that they and their witnesses make on the jury.

How accurate are people in their perceptions of others? This question has been investigated in the context of eyewitness testimony. Evidence is quite conclusive that eyewitness testimony is often inaccurate and full of distortion. Not only is the performance of eyewitnesses in experimental studies quite poor, witnesses to actual crimes have been found to do even more poorly. In one study, a film of a mock crime, a mugging in which a woman's purse was stolen, was shown on a television news show. Shortly afterward, a lineup was shown in which six suspects were on view, one of whom had been the "criminal" in the film. Out of 2,000 people who had seen the mugging on television, over 1,800 identified the wrong man as the criminal or decided incorrectly that none of the six had committed the crime. One third of the witnesses perceived the mugger as being black or Hispanic when, in fact, he was white. Overall, the criminal was identified no more frequently than would be expected by chance by about one in six of the witnesses. The use of slide presentations in the laboratory also obtained no better than chance results in identifying the perpetrator of a crime which had been viewed earlier by subjects.

### § 2-2(B). Perceptual Problems.

To a certain extent, what we take in and what we eliminate from the field of stimuli is controlled by attitudinal factors like those discussed in Chapter 1. On the other hand, much of our perception is involuntary, and much of what we fail to perceive is overlooked by accident. This is because of the nature of the field of stimulation itself. Some stimuli are easy to perceive. Others are difficult to perceive. Some stimuli stand out against a background. Other stimuli blend in.

Anyone who has more than a slight familiarity with jury trials knows that jurors experience many perceptual problems in the courtroom. They can become confused, get witnesses mixed up, and forget important evidence. One reason for this is the overall problem of attention. Jurors are obviously not up on their toes paying rapt attention from the first minute to the closing seconds of a trial. Their minds wander and may even go almost blank for long periods of time. Audio perceptual problems abound. Most of the trial is an exercise in audio communication. In present day society, we are very much conditioned to be visual learners. Studies have shown that visual learning is much more effective than audio learning. When we are listening, we listen much faster than another person can talk. In fact, most people can listen five to seven times faster than a trial lawyer can speak. As we wait to hear more, our mind can drift onto another subject. At that point we miss a few words. Soon we are missing whole sentences and may even stop listening altogether.

There are many reasons why jurors stop listening. A common one, discussed in Chapter 1, is that jurors do not *want* to hear what is being said. But even when they do want to hear it, they may not. They may be forced to stop listening. One reason they may be forced to stop listening is that what they are hearing is so boring that it becomes uncomfortable to listen. Jurors will stop listening and think about something else. Another reason why jurors may stop listening is that they do not understand what they are hearing. It may be too technical and complex, too full of specialized vocabulary and words jurors don't understand. Despite their best intentions, they will stop listening since there is no point in doing so anyway.

Sometimes jurors stop listening because they cannot distinguish what they want to hear from a background of noise. At other times they stop listening because they are preoccupied with something else they cannot get out of their minds. No matter how good a case presentation may be, it will not make an impact on a juror who is not listening.

In addition to audio perceptual problems, there are a host of visual ones. Advertisers, television producers, and other communicators have become adept at promoting visual learning through the use of the theory of sensory perception. Graphic exhibits in trials offer an important opportunity for lawyers to take advantage of this widespread familiarity with visual learning situations. Unfortunately, most graphic exhibits violate the most basic precepts of visual learning. This is usually because exhibits are poorly designed. They are boring, they contain too much detailed information which cannot be clearly separated, and they do not utilize the basic principles of visual communication. Because of common mistakes made in visual communication, jurors often ignore graphic exhibits or fail to understand the message.

## § 2-3. Internal Sets and Distractions.

One of the major reasons for distorted perceptions in the courtroom is the presence of distracting elements within the jurors' minds. In Chapter 1, we saw that jurors often filtered out factual content and testimony when it did not blend in with their attitude sets. Psychologists have also learned that emotional states within people can actually influence what they see when they look at something. Something called "cognitive masking" can occur when a visual display is combined with an emotional stimulus.

In the courtroom, few graphic exhibits are presented in an emotionally neutral context. These exhibits either contain material of a graphic nature toward which jurors feel positive or negative, or the context in which the material is presented creates a positive or negative aura. A video tape of a commercial airline test crash is something that most jurors will not be able to view objectively. Emotional content is obvious. Most people will react by feeling anxious over the fact that anyone in the plane would have been killed or seriously injured. When asked to view the event depicted in the film objectively, many people will have trouble doing so. As a witness discusses the contact between the aircraft and the ground, and notes the precise nature of the damage, some people will have stopped watching and listening. An engineer or a scientist among the jurors will probably continue to listen closely, with interest and curiosity.

In the "cognitive masking" experiments, researchers have shown subjects a number of different symbols. Whenever a particular symbol had strong emotional impact, it tended to mask, or obscure other symbols shown at the same time it was being shown, or just after. Showing pictures of deformed children to pregnant women has had just such an impact.

Post-trial interviews with jurors reveal that cognitive masking does occur in the courtroom.

Let us return to our previous example of the airplane crash. For some jurors, the experience of seeing this film will make such an impact that it will mask everything the witness or attorney says about the film. If an expert analyzes the film, these jurors may tune him out. When the expert is cross-examined, they may not be listening. Their minds may wander back to what they have seen, and the emotional impact it made upon them.

Not only can an emotionally charged visual stimulus block out what comes after, it can even act retrospectively. Experiments have shown that subjects fail to remember visual information that came just before the highly emotionally charged visual stimulus. What this tells us about graphic exhibits in the courtroom is that visual material with strong emotional content may disrupt the way in which jurors are processing information in the trial. It may cause them to forget things that came just before the presentation of the material and to fail to register other information that comes after.

We know what will determine strong emotional reactions to visual material: internal sets. Internal sets are clusters of attitudes, memories of previous behavior and experience, and beliefs and values which can go back to early childhood. Internal sets will vary, of course, from person to person, although large groups of people will display similar internal sets. Jewish people will react with negative emotional responses to the sight of a swastika, for example, as will many non-Jews. How much masking will take place, however, will be an important individual variation. A person who had relatives die in concentration camps will have a very strong negative reaction, may become upset, and thereby miss material which surrounds the view of the swastika. A former concentration camp inmate might well become so upset as to want to leave the room.

Another kind of internal set, besides the emotional-attitudinal one, is called a "perceptual set" by psychologists. Sometimes jurors are expecting to see something. They are set to perceive, or expect to perceive, a particular piece of visual information. They then use this perceptual set to organize what they see. This is not necessarily a problem, but it can be. When a perceptual set is strongly in place and the visual information which is forthcoming is somewhat ambiguous, the influence of the set will be very strong.

Suppose an attorney announces to a jury that they are about to see what happens when a car of a certain make crashes into a block wall at fifty miles an hour. What will jurors expect? Will they expect to see how badly the car fares? How severely it is damaged? Or will they expect to see how well the car withstands the impact? Many kinds of information come in this kind of "half-full/half-empty" form. What is concluded depends on how one wants to see it. That is, of course, precisely the point: jurors do see things the way they want to see them.

The internal sets of jurors are related to a variety of factors. Attitudes and past experiences, as we have noted, can determine many different kinds of internal predispositions to perceive things one way or the other. Sometimes, it is even possible to relate internal sets, or predispositions, to demographic factors, like education, income, and so forth. As we have seen, engineers and scientists have totally different internal sets from those of clerical workers and poets. Furthermore, much of what we have been saying about perceptual problems, cognitive masking, and perceptual sets can also be applied to audio communications. In work at Litigation Sciences where we regularly test attorney opening statements and witness testimony in pretrial settings, we have found these effects operative in both audio and visual communications. Audio masking is common. One emotionally charged item of information can block the recall of what has come before and what will come after, just as it does with a visual communication.

## § 2-4. Signal Detection and Adaptation Level in the Courtroom.

Before we go into the ways in which strategy can be developed to deal with juror perceptional problems, two more perspectives on the matter are worth discussing. These are the theory of signal detection and the concept of adaptation level.

### § 2-4(A). Theory of Signal Detection.

Jurors tune in and tune out during a trial. Most of the time they are in a state of quasi-receptivity after the opening statements are completed. Psychologists who have studied sensory perception have been interested in why people will detect a stimulus one time and not another.

Two answers come immediately to mind. With reference to jurors, they will detect and remember a stimulus if they have sufficient discriminative capacity and if the stimulus is of sufficient magnitude to come to their attention. This is obvious. What is not so obvious, is that jurors only use their discriminative capacity when they feel it is important for them to do so. Psychologists have explained this situation by talking about decision criteria. In other words, jurors have certain criteria they employ which tell them whether or not they want to "detect the signal."

The idea of decision criteria is not difficult to interpret in a trial context. Jurors decide what is worth listening to and what is not in a number of ways. Obviously, they will listen to what goes on at the beginning of a trial because they are getting oriented to a novel situation. They may not be comfortable with their new role as jurors, and they are seeking information. Later, they will already have a fairly clear idea of their verdict, and of course, they will listen to what fits with their interpretation of the case.

Another source of decision criteria employed by jurors in deciding what they ought to be doing at a given point in a trial comes from the attorneys themselves. Is an attorney just going through perfunctory motions in examining a particular witness? Does the judge seem bored? Have spectators in the courtroom gone out for coffee? All of these cues can lead jurors to make a decision that listening at this particular point in the trial is not really very important. They may, for example, begin to think about their daughter's birthday party coming up over the weekend rather than the testimony of an engineering expert on the strength of materials. If, in his testimony, he uses extremely technical terminology and vocabulary which is strange and unfamiliar to the jurors, the decision will probably be to give him only cursory attention.

Finally, on the subject of signal detection, jurors have what is called a low detection threshold when they have the expectation that the stimulus is going to be important. Translated, that means that they will pay attention when they think something important is coming. Finding ways to give them a sense of the importance of what is to come is a basic strategy in dealing with problems of perception in the courtroom.

In short, the theory of signal detection tells us that jurors will adjust their threshold of detection, which is their level of readiness to receive information. They do this according to the strength and uniqueness of the signal, their motivation to receive the signal, and their expectation concerning what the signal will be.

## § 2-4(B). Adaptation Level Theory.

Adaptation level theory, like the theory of signal detection, deals with how jurors comprehend and react to a series of stimuli. Once again, this is a situation typified by a trial. Day after day, jurors sit listening and watching before a steady stream of stimuli. Adaptation level theory tells us that they quickly define what can be called a "neutral frame of reference." Most of what jurors see and hear falls within this neutral frame of reference and does not make strong or necessarily memorable impressions. It is only when a stimulus falls markedly outside this neutral frame of reference that jurors sit up and take notice.

This can be illustrated in the following way. When jurors initially come into the courtroom, their neutral frame of reference is something they have brought with them from outside. Just about everything they experience in the courtroom is markedly outside this frame of reference. Jurors are highly sensitive to everything that is going on. As the hours and days go by, they begin to develop another neutral frame of reference, based on their courtroom experiences. They will have made an adaptation to the trial environment. Almost everything they see and hear will constitute a kind of undifferentiated background, consistent with their neutral frame of reference. Occasionally, something will stand out because of its novelty. Jurors will pay attention to this novel stimulus. The juror is in a position not unlike a subject in a research experiment who is shown a succession of red cards. The twenty-seventh card will be yellow, and the balance of the cards will be red, up to the total of one hundred. When asked immediately what they remember, the subjects in such an experiment will say they remember the yellow card.

## § 2-5. Strategies.

At Litigation Sciences, we have developed a number of strategic approaches and techniques for dealing with the perceptual problems of jurors. These involve the application of the kinds of ideas we have been discussing in the first part of this chapter.

### § 2-5(A). Commanding and Maintaining Attention.

Attention is the basic state of receptivity. In order for perception to occur, attention must be aroused. As we have suggested, there are many times during the trial when jurors are not paying attention. There are a number of things that can be done about this.

We have introduced three basic experimental perspectives: internal sets, signal detection, and adaptation level. All of these point to the same conclusion. Jurors will have the highest level of attention, perceive the most, and remember the most, at the beginning of the trial. This means that the opening of the trial offers a unique opportunity to communicate with jurors. Everything that is done in voir dire and in the opening statement will make a strong impression on jurors. It is novel, and jurors will not have established a neutral frame of reference. Nor will they have developed their own decision criteria for when they should listen and when it is not necessary to do so. Now they will be listening all the time. Because of this, it is a basic trial strategy to place a great deal of attention on voir dire and the opening statement.

This does not mean, however, that we concede the impossibility of continuing to communicate with jurors after the opening statement. On the contrary, it is most important to do so. Attorneys can use movements, gestures, and voice to arouse a juror's attention. Variation is extremely important. Addressing the jury in a different tone of voice or from a different place in the courtroom can break up an ebb in attention. A continual variation of the speaking level, as well as the use of dramatic gestures and dramatic inflections, will be useful. Most of all, attorneys should try to avoid sounding bored themselves. They must avoid a business-as-usual monotone.

Deciding how to position important information in the trial is also of the greatest importance. As noted, the beginning of the trial is an ideal time to lay out the most important points in the case, such as Psychological Anchors. Later, there will be other times when it is propitious to impart critical facts. In part, it is a question of avoiding the worst times.

The adage "depositions are deadly" illustrates what we mean by one of the worst times. A deluge of dull depos will establish a very high threshold of signal detection on the part of jurors. Their perceptual decision criteria will tell them that "this is not worth listening to." Trying to make important points at this time would be a mistake. If there is critical information in the depositions, it will have to be differentiated by some change of reference such as changing the rate of reading, having someone new read, or having something distinctive or different about the reader. An example may be utilizing a young female to read the deposition responses of a senior male executive. Often, in post-trial interviews, jurors will indicate that an attorney's most important arguments went right by them. They don't even remember hearing them. This may have been because the points were contained in a deposition or some dull witness testimony to which jurors were not paying attention.

Key witnesses must also be presented at key times. After a recess is a time when jurors are normally paying attention. They may also be paying attention if reporters show up in the courtroom. In other words, if the witness is important, attorneys must do everything possible to insure that the jury is listening.

### § 2-5(B). Making the Communication "Stick."

We may succeed in arousing the jury's attention, but that still does not mean that the act of perception will be successful and that the communication will stick in a juror's memory. Here, knowledge of the internal sets of jurors will be very important. These can often be understood at least in part by careful examination of Juror Attitude Survey research results. Knowing who our jurors are will be extremely helpful in forming strategy in how to communicate with them. Often, language and communication style can be tailored to juror types. Scientists, engineers, and accountants are likely to respond well to logic and detail. They may tune out emotional arguments and subjective approaches of almost any kind. People with little education, strong religious commitments, and extreme political orientation will tend to place emphasis on emotions and feelings in judging a communication. If jurors who prove to be predisposed to our side are mainly of the first type, we will lean more heavily on highly detailed and logical arguments in presenting the case than with jurors of the second type.

There are many distinctions like these which can provide guideposts for communication. Often these are closely related to the venue and represent geographic and demographic differences. One does not communicate in New York City in the same style one communicates in Harlan County, Kentucky.

Sometimes, an expectancy set will be in place which represents a fairly general norm, even cutting across regions. Medical professors who are acting as expert witnesses will be expected to appear and comport themselves in a particular manner. There will be some regional variation in what jurors expect, but it will be within a known range. Such a witness should be very neat and fastidious, articulate, judicious, aloof in some ways, but with a kind of undercurrent of warmth indicative of bedside compassion. The precise way in which these ingredients should play and be combined will be subject to regional differences.

There are many credibility issues that will be important in communication. At this point, it is well to remember that if we want to deal effectively with jurors' perceptual problems, we must command their attention. Once we have it, we must bring forward an effective communication, adequate to their expectations, and suitable to their attitudes and style of thinking. This may sound elementary, but in practice it takes a great deal of work to achieve.

## § 2-6. Strategy for Graphic Exhibits.

The world we live in is increasingly oriented toward the visual. Jurors are accustomed to receiving important information through visual means. From traffic signals and road signs to the myriad advertisements in magazines and on television, jurors use visually obtained information as a basis for decisions and actions. For people under the age of forty, television has usually been the primary source of learning and information. It has been estimated that upon graduation, the average high school student has completed 11,000 hours of classroom education while viewing over 15,000 hours of television.

Because of their physical makeup as human beings acting together with cultural traits, jurors are essentially visual learners. Experiments have shown that when information is presented to us through audio means we retain only about 10 percent of what we hear. Contrast this with the fact that we retain 85 percent of what we learn visually.

This points to the importance of graphic exhibits in the courtroom, an importance often overlooked. Psychologists and graphic artists have studied the factors in perception which determine how a graphic display will be perceived and remembered. Knowledge of these factors can be applied to the design of effective graphic exhibits.

### § 2-6(A). Gestalt Grouping: Figure-Ground.

The essential problem in visual perception involves how well jurors can perceive a figure against a background. In an effective communication, the salient information always stands out. This is particularly true of visual communications in court.

People perceive figures against a background because they have a tendency to organize what they see. The way this organizing tendency operates will depend on the features of the graphic design before us. The term "gestalt" is the German word for form or shape. Gestalt grouping principles are those principles through which jurors see figure-like qualities and group relationships in visual perceptions.

Gestalt psychologists have worked with elements in the visual design itself. These elements include color, size, contrast and contour, luminance, depth, movement, and pattern. All of these elements can be manipulated to make the design a better communication. Combining colors and shapes can often produce subjective effects which draw jurors to conclusions they would not otherwise reach upon looking at the display. Key facts in a chain of apparently undifferentiated information can be made to stand out. In all of this, our objective will be to translate dry facts and numbers into a visual learning device which will communicate in a powerful way.

## § 2-6(B). Pretesting Graphic Exhibits.

It is a curious fact of litigation that so much can be at risk in the courtroom, and yet some attorneys continue to come before a jury with an untested product. Business, in general, has developed the practice of conducting considerable research and testing before important product decisions are made. There is good reason to extend this practice to the law. One of the easiest elements in a lawyer's case to pretest is the graphic exhibit. Graphic exhibits can be prepared well in advance of the trial and tested extensively before surrogate jurors. Through this kind of research, lawyers can often learn how effective a graphic exhibit will be in terms of its design on the one hand and juror internal sets on the other. In some cases, we have discovered through pretrial research that jurors have negative emotional reactions to certain exhibits which cause the exhibits to be distorted or ignored. It is also possible to evaluate whether or not the exhibit conveys the information we would like it to convey. In addition, we can also learn from experiments in an extended time frame how well the content of the graphic will be remembered.

## § 2-6(C). What Should A Good Graphic Exhibit Do?

A number of different criteria have been developed for evaluating the effectiveness of visual evidence. These can be stated as rules for the production of exhibits and graphic displays.

The first rule to bear in mind is that exhibits must convey a clear and understandable message, and the message must provide instantaneous meaning. Just as drivers do not back up on freeways to read messages on billboards, jurors do not typically ponder and study a stream of displays in a courtroom. For the most part, they simply will not have time to ponder. They will be put off by an exhibit that asks too much of them and are likely to invoke the kind of decision criteria we have spoken of earlier — they may decide the exhibit is not worth bothering with. The moment for an exhibit must be seized aggressively. The message must be conveyed in an instant.

Secondly, an exhibit must be simple and straightforward. It cannot present too much information at one time. The attention and perceptual problems experienced by jurors must be addressed by simplification. If the information is too complex, jurors will override the information being given, and it will be tuned out.

Third, exhibits are enhanced by the proper use of cues. Cues can come before a display or just after. Cues given just before a graphic display is seen, or just as it is being seen, are signposts pointing out what is significant in the exhibit. It is important that jurors know what they are being shown and why. Cues can also come after an exhibit has been seen. These after-cues are very important. Research has shown that visual memory is fleeting. After any visual perception, there is a brief period during which a great deal about the perception will be recalled. This information should be reinforced at once.

Fourth, graphic exhibits must be presented in a context that is free from extraneous and distracting information. This rule follows from the fact that people normally receive more information than they can process. Psychologists have identified something called the "cocktail party phenomenon." This phenomenon can be expressed quite simply. In a crowded room at a party, there are numerous conversations in progress. A person may have difficulty concentrating on a single focal conversation of interest. This situation can be generalized to all perception.

Jurors must constantly deal with the fact that they perceive more information than they can use. One way of looking at the issue of distraction is to view it as a shifting back and forth between what is focal and what is not focal. Jurors are prone to this kind of "mind-wandering" when they are being talked at or shown something. A critical problem for an attorney at all times, and particularly with regard to a demonstrative exhibit, is to see that the jury's attention is focused on the one channel through which the attorney's message is being transmitted. There should be no distractions. The exhibit itself should contain no ambiguous elements or eye-catching effects that are not directly related to the message.

Finally, it is important to remember that jurors pay attention to what they like. Successful exhibits must be appealing. In the past, many attorneys have expressed concern about juror backlash if a graphic exhibit is "too slick." This appears to be a myth. It is not borne out by what jurors themselves report.

There are a number of ways in which jurors find graphic exhibits appealing. To begin with, they like things which are easy to grasp. Visual displays can be made more accessible to jurors by utilizing the jurors' own experiences. As we have seen in our discussion of perceptual sets, previous experience is important in any perception. Whether or not jurors will perceive the message in a graphic display may depend on whether or not it is recognizable to them. Whenever objects which are familiar to jurors are used in demonstrative exhibits, we will have a better chance of commanding their attention and getting the message across.

Visual exhibits can also be made appealing by using elements which produce a high level of sensory excitation. Whenever possible, an exhibit should generate visually exciting effects. Often, this can be achieved through the use of bold and distinctive shapes and colors, the use of contrast, or cleverly drawn familiar objects.

## § 2-7. Conclusions.

When we think of attention problems in the courtroom, we tend to think offensively. How can we make sure jurors are paying attention when we have the floor? Lawyers should be constantly engaged in attempts to arouse and hold attention. They can vary the number of lawyers in the courtroom, vary the lawyers who are conducting examinations, alter communication style, insert particularly effective and interesting witnesses at key moments, and use psychologically appealing visual displays and exhibits. These techniques can contribute to success in keeping the attention of jurors at a receptive level.

But what if we do not want jurors to pay attention? Suppose the opposition is about to call a key witness. Here the strategy of distraction can be very important. We may want to load the courtroom with a number of spectators who have never been in court before. We might bring in another member of our own staff who is physically prepossessing and who will attract attention. This person will merely sit and not become involved in cross-examination. He will constitute a distraction, directing attention away from the witness by being passive but very much present. Were this person to examine the witness, then his presence in the courtroom would become connected with the presence of the witness and reinforce the importance of this witness. The famous alleged paper clip and cigar ash of William Jennings Bryan was such a passive distraction device. The cigar ash was calculated to mesmerize the jury into a fascination with its increasing length. Bryan's constant fiddling with a paper clip was a similar distraction.

When an effective distraction is in progress, jurors may think they are listening to the witness, but when the trial is over, they typically will not remember what they heard. Their attention was divided and unfocused. No effective communication was taking place.

Overall, communication experts will advise attorneys to be aware of how to make salient parts of their own case presentation stand out. Likewise, it is useful to know how to make salient parts of the opposing case presentation blend in.

But isn't all of our case salient? In a way it is, but not to jurors. Much of what attorneys want to introduce into the case presentation is important from a legal standpoint, particularly with respect to judges' rulings and the possibilities for appeal. But it is not all salient to jurors, and we will be well advised to know just what is. Otherwise, our entire case presentation may come across as dull and unfocused, if it comes across at all.

# CHAPTER 3

## HOW JURORS FIX BLAME: BASING STRATEGY ON CAUSAL ATTRIBUTION



Lawsuits occur because the plaintiff feels that some sequence of events has taken place which has resulted in a blamable injury. The plaintiff is going to ask the jurors to find the defendant at fault. Jurors are brought into the courtroom to judge the sequence of events, to hear both parties argue about what happened, and ultimately to decide whether anyone is to blame.

## § 3-1. Blame: Attributing Intent and Motivation to Another Person's Behavior.

Behavioral scientists know a great deal about how jurors attribute blame. We also have an excellent model of how they judge and evaluate a sequence of events with a view to deciding what has caused what.

One of the most basic things a juror does when hearing a case is to try to put together an organized, meaningful explanation of what has happened. The drive to do this stems from a natural impulse to understand and control our own immediate environment, so that we can limit the impact of unpredictable and uncontrollable situations. This need is particularly great among jurors in cases in which there has been a tragedy of some kind. This is often true, for example, of product liability cases, or negligence cases in which serious injury or death has occurred. As a consequence of their need to make unpleasant and sometimes tragic situations comprehensible, and hence not totally beyond anyone's control, jurors look for cause and effect patterns. They want to explain what happened in a way that will allow them to be reassured that such a thing will not happen to them. In looking for cause and effect patterns, they attempt to evaluate the defendant's role in some possible sequence of causes. In assessing the defendant's role, jurors do one other thing. They also assess the defendant.

When people judge any situation, they judge the human actors involved. We decide whether or not what happened was the actor's fault, or due to circumstances beyond the actor's control. If it is determined that it is the actor's fault, we ask whether someone acted the way he did because of the situation he was in, or because of the kind of person he is.

It may be supposed that jurors attribute blame, intent, and motivation after a careful, objective assessment of the matter. Some jurors probably do. But in our experience, those who do form a minority. Psychologists have tested what they call "cognitive attributional abilities." The results of this research indicate that people tend to muddle through judgments, and are quite inept at all but the simplest inferential tasks. One of the problems jurors have in making attributions is characteristic of their general perceptual and information processing problems. Jurors, like the subjects of several well-known studies, are often wrong in their recollection and prediction of events. This is largely because no matter how conscientious they may be, they are confronted with more information than they are able to process.

## § 3-2. Basing Strategy on Attribution Theory.

Through the use of small group research, it is possible to learn what attributions jurors are likely to make. We must know, however, what we are looking for. There are several different perspectives in the attribution theory used by social psychologists which can be applied to the problems of trial strategy. Two of the most useful will be discussed here: co-variation theory and the theory of causal schemata.

### § 3-2(A). Co-Variation as a Basis for Attribution.

The notion of co-variation is really quite simple. When jurors want to test their ideas about a person's intent and motivation, they will sometimes examine the person's behavior under a number of conditions and try to work out what factors go together, or co-vary. In this way they will look for a trend that will lead them to a cause and effect explanation of the individual's behavior.

Jurors use the principle of co-variation to make judgments about both internal and external motivation. Knowledge of this fact gives us a basis for developing strategy.

## § 3-2(B). Distinctiveness, Consensus, and Consistency.

Internal attribution occurs when jurors blame the defendant or the plaintiff for an outcome on the basis of that person's character alone. External attribution, on the other hand, is the judgment that the behavior took place because of the situation, or the circumstances. How do jurors reach such conclusions? One of the ways they do so is by trying to discover if the person they are judging always acts the way he or she was alleged to have acted in this case. Let's look at this from the perspective of a defendant. Jurors will ask themselves, and each other in deliberation, if the defendant always acts this way.

If the defendant seems at all times to act the way he is alleged to have acted in the case, then jurors will have a tendency to think the cause of the behavior lies inside the person. They will make an internal attribution. If the evidence indicates that the defendant does not usually act this way, then jurors will be more inclined to attribute what happened to external circumstances. Thus, if the behavior is high in distinctiveness, it will probably be interpreted in terms of an external attribution.

Jurors use a consensus criterion in a similar way. They will look at the plaintiff or defendant and ask themselves do other people act this way under similar circumstances? If the answer is yes, they will be inclined to make an external attribution. The circumstances are to blame. If they conclude that other people do not act in such a manner, then they will incline toward an internal attribution. The person is to blame. Is the behavior high in consensus? Does everyone do it? Or is it unique, that is, low in consensus?

A consistency criterion is also employed. Here, another time dimension is invoked. Is a person's behavior consistent over time, or does it show inconsistencies? Obviously, consistent behavior points to an internal motivation. The action has taken place because of the way the person is. If, however, there is a lot of inconsistency in the actions under review, an external attribution is more likely.

Jurors are inclined to use something like co-variation thinking when there is a strong time dimension in the trial. If it is a question of evaluating how many separate actions over a long period of time can be construed as a whole, they'll find co-variation thinking useful. Co-variation thinking can also be used in evaluating a single action.

The latter can be seen in a case involving a recently deceased driver whose family is in court as the plaintiff. One of the issues in this case will be the decedent's history as a driver. In a more general sense, his history as a human being might also be an issue.

Is having an accident a distinctive event for this driver, or has he had a lot of accidents? If an attorney can convince jurors that this accident is distinctive, a first-time occurrence, there will be a greater tendency among jurors to attribute the accident to external circumstances. The consensus criterion can also be employed. A close study of what happened will lead jurors to decide whether or not other people would have acted the same way. Did the driver make an unusual panic move? Does the evidence (skid marks, witnesses, etc.), point to the conclusion that the driver did no more and no less than any other normal person would have done under the circumstances? If so, the jurors again would lean toward an external attribution.

Consistency can also come into play. Suppose the plaintiff argues that the steering locked. In fact, the car left a high speed curve rated at 45 miles per hour, rolled over in a ditch, and finally came to rest at impact against a pole. The jurors are evaluating a proposition. Was the driver a person who liked to take risks? Was he a thrill seeker? Would he have tried taking the curve at 60 miles per hour, just to see what it felt like? Was his life a life of seeking "highs," "kicks," living in the fast lane, on the edge? No, the plaintiff argues. The man was conservative and prudent in all that he did. His driving pattern was consistent with everything he did. Regardless of the activity, the time, the circumstances, his approach was always the same — even-handed, judicious, moderate. If the jurors accept the plaintiff's argument, they will once again look for a way to make an external attribution.

## § 3-2(C). Basing Strategy on Co-Variation.

We can use research to learn when jurors are going to use co-variation thinking in judging a case. Once we have clues as to how jurors will make attributions using co-variation, it will be relatively easy to formulate strategy. Attorneys can use the criteria of distinctiveness, consensus, and consistency to help jurors see the litigant's role as something dictated by external factors, or if need be, factors inside the person. As we have seen, this is very important in a number of different kinds of trials. Here is another illustration.

A young lady who is a Manhattan socialite is "kidnapped" by a terrorist group. Apparently acting with them and of her own free will, she is photographed in the act of robbing a bank. Later she is apprehended and tried for this crime. Her attorneys make the following claims:

1. Her behavior is high in distinctiveness. She has never robbed a bank before. She has never stolen anything.
2. Her behavior is high in consensus. With a gun at your head, what would you do? Anyone would have done the same thing under the circumstances.
3. Her behavior is consistent. The defendant is an obedient, well-mannered, dutiful young woman, looking out for her own survival.

Since the defendant's behavior is high in distinctiveness, high in consensus, and high in consistency, the cause of this behavior must have been external circumstances, beyond her control.

But, the prosecutor argues:

1. Her behavior is low in distinctiveness. She was caught shoplifting at the age of seventeen, and she once attended a peace rally at which one of the terrorists made a speech. For her, robbing a bank in the company of terrorists is not particularly distinctive.
2. Her behavior is not high in consensus, it is low in consensus. Normal people would not be brandishing automatic weapons in front of bank tellers, no matter what the circumstances.
3. Her behavior is high in consistency, as the plaintiff argues, but consistent with what? She has always been an unruly and troubled child. She has been in trouble in school, and was once rounded up by the police for drinking beer under the age of eighteen in Washington Park.

Ergo, the prosecutor argues, the young socialite's behavior is low in distinctiveness, low in consensus, and high in consistency. She robbed the bank because of who she was, and not because of the external circumstances.

Of course, the above is a simplification, but it contains the general idea. Using co-variation strategy will depend on a good research effort aimed at discovering which issues the trial jurors will find important. After that, the specific ways in which co-variation thinking will come into play must be worked out. When this is done, specific strategic approaches, both offensive and defensive, can be formulated.

## § 3-2(D). Attribution by Causal Schemata as a Basis for Strategy.

Co-variation thinking is pretty sophisticated for jurors, who, as we have noted, may not be very analytic or inferential. Co-variation thinking will appeal to certain jurors more than others. That's why pretrial investigation into juror profiles is so important. It will tell us, among other things, whether or not jurors predisposed to our side are likely to think in terms of attribution based on co-variation.

Another simpler, more naive way of making attributions is through the use of causal schemata. Causal schemata enable people to translate attitude and experiential constellations directly into attributions. They also sometimes lead directly to the discovery of Psychological Anchors, the key issues jurors will use to make their decision.

A causal schema is a sort of script jurors use to make sense out of events. Such schemata are based on the storehouse of attitudes and beliefs jurors bring with them into the courtroom. People are accustomed to making hundreds of causal attributions every day. We are constantly explaining to ourselves why a certain event has occurred. We are also constantly making implicit judgments about people. Causal schemata are the short formulas we use to make quick inferences. They come into play whenever we see certain cues in our environment. If jurors see two attorneys conferring outside the courtroom, for example, they reach conclusions about what is going on by observing how the attorneys look. If one seems to be annoyed with his younger colleague, who in turn looks a little chagrined, the jurors may reach the conclusion that something adverse has occurred in the conduct of the case. The older attorney is blaming it on his younger colleague.

Jurors are constantly making causal attributions by means of causal schemata. They do so with regard to all the actors in the courtroom — judge, other jurors, attorneys, witnesses, and litigants. It is important to be aware of this fact, and to deal with its implications.

Making attributions by means of causal schemata is a common way for jurors to deal with evidence. We recently dealt with a product liability case in which a child suffered birth defects. The plaintiff argued that the birth defects were the result of the mother's prenatal exposure to certain household products which contained toxic chemicals. One of the objectives we pursued in pretrial research was to try to determine what kind of attitudes people held who were strongly predisposed toward the plaintiff. There were a number of factors involved in constructing a profile of the typical plaintiff juror. One of the most interesting involved a causal schema. We discovered that the large number of people we surveyed on this case divided into two groups — those who thought they could routinely tell the cause of a birth defect, and those who thought they could not. The best predictor of plaintiff sympathies was the "can tell" characteristic. When this "can tell" trait was found in combination with certain other key characteristics, we had the "perfect" plaintiff juror. Since we were working with the defendants in this case, this was a juror we wanted to avoid at all costs.

The "can tell" causal schema in the birth defect case seemed to work in a fairly straightforward manner. The environmental cue was that a birth defect had taken place. The jurors who possessed the "can tell" causal schema immediately took the position that we ought to be able to find out what caused the defect. They were quite willing to accept whatever happened to be "up to bat at the moment" as the cause. In our surveys, we presented a number of potential causative factors, such as genetics, exposure to pesticides, exposure to pharmaceuticals, as well as a number of contrived, far-reaching explanations. These jurors were willing to accept any of these causes.

The jurors who had the "can't tell" schema in place reacted differently to the same environmental cue, the presence of a birth defect. They believed that it is very difficult, if not impossible, to ever know specifically what caused such defects. They regarded with skepticism arguments positing plaintiff's causal explanations.

We need not belabor the point. Obviously, when empirical research uncovers the presence of causal schemata in the jurors' decision-making process, these schemata must be taken seriously and used as a basis for forming trial strategy.

## § 3-3. Defensive Attribution: Specific Strategy.

One of the areas of specific jury trial strategy which is based upon relatively recent theoretical development is that of defensive attribution. A great deal of product liability and negligence litigation involves accidents. Attribution theory is a particularly useful way to approach these cases. The ideal defense in a case involving an accident is to persuade the jurors to hold the accident victim responsible for his or her plight. Psychologists have discovered that observers are often inclined to hold accident victims responsible for what has happened to them. They do so because of a phenomenon called defensive attribution.

In studying defensive attribution, researchers have sought to identify relationships between the victim and the observers. In the case of jurors, we might ask how the difference in age between the juror and the victim will affect the attribution process. Will attribution vary with the intensity of the accident? Does blaming the victim depend upon a feeling of identification with the victim on the part of the juror? Research has shown that if a juror perceives the victim to be like himself on some significant dimension, he may blame the victim. Why does this happen?

When a juror becomes familiar with the facts of an accident, there is a psychological tendency to worry about being involved in a similar situation. This concern can be increased dramatically to the extent that the juror identifies with the victim. They may have similar backgrounds. The juror may have engaged in similar activities. They may be the same sex and age. Psychologically, jurors will need to deal with this concern. They will need to find reasons why what happened to the victim could not happen to them. Their view of reality is that they are normally safe from such accidents. Now they have learned that such an accident has occurred, and the person involved is similar to themselves. They need to cope defensively with this fact.

One way to cope with an anxiety-provoking event, which has happened to someone else, is to neutralize the possible impact of blind fate, or uncontrollable outside forces, and blame the victim. It happened to him, because he is such and such a person who did such and such a thing, but it would not happen to me because I would not do that. So the reasoning goes.

## § 3-3(A). The Intensity Factor.

Researchers have measured the effect of varying the intensity of the accident on defensive attribution. It has been found that people will assign increasing responsibility to the victim as the intensity of the accident increases. When the accident is less severe, people will tend to release the victim from responsibility.

What about the identification factor? If an observer identifies strongly with the victim in the case of a very severe accident, the likelihood of blaming the victim is increased even further. The implication that the observer may also suffer a grave accident is more threatening. By blaming the victim and stressing that he is a different kind of person, the observer can psychologically insulate himself from the threat of being involved in a similar disaster.

## § 3-3(B). A Case Example.

Litigation Sciences has conducted specific research into the defensive attribution phenomenon. One study used two principal questions as lines of inquiry. The first was, "Will a potential juror assign a greater responsibility to a victim of an accident if he perceives a strong possibility that the accident could happen to himself?" The second question was, "Do the ages of potential juror and victim interact in some way with respect to the blame factor?"

### § 3-3(B)(1). The Study.

In a telephone survey with over 1,000 participants, answers were sought to these questions. The venue was an area in northeastern United States where a trial involving a serious accident was about to take place.

Study subjects were read a test scenario describing: (1) the accident; (2) the driver who was referred to as "Jim"; and (3) the nature and consequences of his injuries. Some of the questions subjects were asked included:

1. How responsible was Jim for the accident?
2. How careless was Jim?
3. Did Jim do enough to avoid the accident?
4. Was the accident due to chance?
5. How likely is it that this accident could have happened to you?
6. From the little you know about Jim, do you think he's the same kind of person you are?
7. Do you have a relative or a close friend who is like Jim?
8. Would you like Jim as a friend?
9. Would you trust Jim?

We also collected information about the people who participated in the study. The majority were over 25 years of age, Caucasian, and politically conservative or moderate. Their occupations were distributed broadly across employment categories. There were relatively few technical, professional, or entrepreneurially-oriented respondents in our sample.

### § 3-3(B)(2). The Age Factor.

Jim's age was varied in the accident scenario described to the subjects in the study. We found no connection, however, between the answers to the nine questions listed above and the extent to which Jim's age did or did not correspond to the age of the respondent.

### § 3-3(B)(3). The Identification Factor.

Here, there were highly significant correlations. The answers to the questions were given on a three point scale: *very much, some, not at all* (with grammatical modifications for the different questions). We separated the group of respondents who answered "very likely" when asked: "How likely is it that this accident could have happened to you?" We then examined how many of these people thought Jim was responsible for the accident. Jurors who thought the accident could have happened to them were the same ones who found Jim responsible. This group also thought that Jim had been careless and did not think the accident had been the result of chance factors. For those people who thought "it can happen to me," the victim of the accident was blamed and held responsible.

### § 3-3(B)(4). Strategies for Voir Dire Based on Defensive Attribution.

What are the implications of our study results from a defense strategy perspective? Suppose the defendant is the governmental agency responsible for maintaining the road. Plaintiff alleges that the shoulder was poorly maintained, that the outside stripe marking the edge of the pavement was too indistinct, and that the road grade itself was improperly designed and unsafe. We want a jury who will blame Jim for what happened. To begin with, we want jurors who think a similar accident might happen to them. Voir dire questions, then, might be designed to find out whether or not a juror engages in behavior similar to Jim's. Is there anything we can learn about jurors which would indicate that they might find themselves in a similar situation? Do they travel the same road as the plaintiff? Do they travel at the same time of the night? Are their driving habits similar? Do they, or would they, drive at the same speed? Would they operate their automobile the same way under similar circumstances? Can we find jurors who regularly travel in the early morning at speeds in excess of 60 miles per hour? Can we find jurors who drive similar cars?

While jurors who believe that they could have a similar accident will make good defense jurors, we must be wary of jurors who have already had a similar accident. The latter will sympathize with the victim.

Consistent with defensive attribution theory, a juror who thinks he or she could personally have such an accident will possess a deep need to rationalize the situation. This rationalization must lead to the ultimate conclusion that such an accident would not occur with the juror as driver. In order for this conviction to stick, the juror must identify characteristics of the victim which explain what happened. If the juror drives a similar car over a similar route at a similar time of day, he must find a unique fault with the plaintiff indicative of human error.

In voir dire, the defense will want to explain the situation, then ask prospective jurors if they have ever been involved in a similar accident. The prospective jurors can then be asked whether or not they think the accident could have happened to them. Through the use of such questions, attorneys for the defense should be able to identify jurors who are likely to be positively or negatively disposed toward the defendant. Plaintiffs, of course, will want to know the same information. Plaintiffs will want jurors who are unlikely to blame the victim.

From a defensive attribution perspective, defense lawyers should also make reference to items or events identified in voir dire which are of significance in the jurors' lives. For example, if defense counsel learn from voir dire that the vehicle involved in the accident is similar to a juror's, the attorney should go to some length to describe the car in detail. This sort of thing should be particularly aimed at defense-oriented jurors.

## § 3-4. "Compliance With Standards" Defense: An Application of Attribution Theory.

Another way in which trial strategy can be based on attribution theory can be illustrated by the compliance with standards defense in product liability trials. In product liability actions, the defense may be inclined to base its case at least in part upon the fact that the defendant has been in compliance with some private organization or public agency that has established standards for quality and safety as they apply to the product in question. Such a defense raises problems which can only be addressed by attitude and attribution theory. This chapter will conclude with a discussion as to why this strategy is one of the more problematic approaches the defense can pursue in product liability cases.

The attribution aspect of a compliance with standards defense is twofold. First, the jury will evaluate the defendant on the basis of whether or not the act of being in compliance with certain standards is enough to make the defendant a "good," "responsible," or "honest" manufacturer of the product. In other words, what kind of reflection is it upon the defendant to have been in compliance with standards? What kind of attributions will be made as a result of compliance? Further, what kind of negative attributions will be made with regard to defendants found not to be in compliance with standards?

The second way in which attribution becomes germane in these cases concerns perceptions of the organizations which establish standards. What kind of attributions will jurors make about a government agency, an industry association, a private research foundation, or a research and standards institute associated with a large university? Are jurors impressed by any or all of these organizations? What sort of attributions do jurors begin to make when the name of a particular organization is invoked?

The attributions jurors make in the case of compliance versus non-compliance with standards are also linked to juror attitudes. We might suppose, for example, that jurors with initial negative attitudes toward industry and business will be more impressed with compliance than jurors who do not harbor such negative attitudes. We might discover other kinds of attitudes which are relevant, such as attitudes and beliefs about the standard-setting organizations themselves. We would not normally expect a juror with a strong anti-government bias to be impressed with a firm which had been in compliance with standards set by a government agency.

Attributions with regard to compliance with standards may also be correlated with demographic factors. Do the sex and age of jurors make a difference? Do income or education matter? All of these questions must be answered before a strategy involving compliance defense can be evaluated.

## § 3-4(A). A Case Study.

In order to develop some general orientation toward this strategy, Litigation Sciences carried out an investigation using a number of fictitious scenarios which involved typical products cases in the automobile and pharmaceutical industries. In each of these areas, we knew that traditionally there have been large compensatory and punitive awards and that defendants have often relied heavily on the compliance defense. In each of these test scenarios, defendants had either met or failed to meet government or industry-set product standards.

The initial hypothesis in the study was to test whether or not a defendant's compliance would be an important factor in jurors' minds. From an attribution theory perspective, it was felt that if a defendant had been in compliance, jurors would be less willing to attribute the harm which plaintiff suffered entirely to the defendant's actions. In contrast, when the defendant had not been in compliance, it was supposed that jurors would see the cause of injury associated with the defendant's behavior. Just about all of these assumptions were soundly refuted by the data.

## § 3-4(B). Research Findings on Compliance Attributions.

On a scale measuring approval, with "1" being low and "8" being high, the highest score that a defendant received who had been in compliance with specific manufacturing standards was about 4.5. This related to government agency standards. At best, it was discovered that jurors were not impressed with claims of compliance with government standards. Compliance with these standards did not lead jurors to make positive attributions where defendants were being evaluated. Where industry standards were at issue, compliance was even less of a factor in favorably impressing jurors. Here, there was strong evidence that a defense based on compliance would elicit no more than a neutral reaction among jurors. These neutral reactions would not be sufficient to induce the desired external attribution, that is, the attribution that the harm to plaintiff occurred as a result of factors outside the defendant's control.

Based on these findings, one might suppose that when a defendant has not complied with standards, it will not matter much to jurors. Not so. When the defendant is a non-complier, evidence suggests that jurors will be quick to form a negative opinion. In fact, non-compliance has potentially disastrous consequences for the defendant. On the same approval rating scale of 1 to 8, defendants in a non-compliance scenario score very low and were regarded unfavorably by jurors. There is reason to believe that if the plaintiff pursues a strategy of demonstrating that the defendant is in non-compliance with established standards, defense counsel will have a difficult time bringing jurors up to a position of mere neutrality toward their client on this issue. Jurors will readily make damaging internal attributions associating injury or damage with the defendant's non-complying behavior.

Do these attributions, which vary from negative to neutral, merely reflect pre-existing negative attitudes? In order to assess this factor, jurors were asked a series of questions about corporations in general. Based on the answers to these questions, jurors were classified as either pro-business or anti-business. Jurors who were classified as anti-business exhibited extremely negative attitudes toward product liability defendants who were not in compliance with industry and government standards. This is not particularly surprising. However, pro-business jurors displayed an equally negative attitude toward non-complying defendants. In fact, when pro-business jurors were asked to evaluate a pharmaceutical defendant who was not in compliance with government standards, they made an extremely negative evaluation, even more negative than that made by the group of anti-industry jurors. Apparently, the pro-business group made such a negative attribution precisely because they held a pro-business predisposition and were incensed by what they regarded as the defendant's "breach of faith."

Thus, there seems to be little difference between pro-business and anti-business jurors when it comes to making negative attributions toward product liability defendants when the issue of compliance with standards is raised. What differences there are seem to indicate that jurors with pro-business attitudes in place are harder on the non-complying defendant than anti-business jurors. Overall, it was discovered that initial juror predispositions or biases and the nature of the industry, either automobile or pharmaceutical, make little difference in the way attributions are made where compliance with standards is an issue.

## § 3-4(C). The Two Strategies of Enhancement and Denial.

Given the way in which jurors make attributions when the matter of compliance with standards comes up in a trial, there are two basic strategies which can be followed: enhancement and denial. When a defendant wishes to employ compliance with standards as part of an overall trial strategy, it will be necessary to "enhance" the importance of meeting standards in the minds of the jurors. This is so because, as we have seen, jurors generally are not overly impressed with the fact that a product liability defendant has been in compliance with standards set by some testing agency. On the other hand, when plaintiffs make the argument that non-compliance with standards is significant, the defendant must deny the importance of these standards. The same strategies, enhancement and denial, can be pursued by the plaintiff. When the plaintiff attacks the defendant for non-compliance, the importance of the standard which has not been met should be emphasized. When the defendant is using compliance as a line of defense, the plaintiff can pursue a strategy of denying that the standard has any real significance.

Using denial and enhancement strategies effectively will involve knowing how jurors make attributions regarding organizations which set standards. These perceptions are important. Research has shown that jurors make very different kinds of attributions relating to these various groups, agencies, or organizations.

Knowing what we do about how jurors evaluate organizations which establish standards can also tell us when not to attack them. Jurors invariably rank consumer protection groups and university research centers as very effective in setting standards and measuring compliance. This rating is so strong that an attorney who attacks these groups may very well compromise his own credibility. Standards set by major corporations and industry trade groups are regarded as quite ineffective by jurors. Attacking such standards, or denying that they have any real importance, is much more likely to win favor. Thus, the success or failure of a compliance defense will depend in part upon the agency involved. Compliance with organizations like consumer protection groups, university research centers, and independent testing laboratories will be more effective in persuading jurors, and this kind of compliance should be emphasized. If compliance with government and industry agencies figures highly in the defendant's behavior, then an effort must be made to show that these standards mean something. In general, when it is necessary to emphasize a client's adherence to standards, the proper procedure is to point to the professionalism, scientific thoroughness, and prestige of the specific agency involved. It can never be taken for granted that the public in general, and jurors in particular, will have a positive image of any standards-setting organization. Of course, when the importance of standards is going to be denied, the image, reputation, or effectiveness of the agency in question can be challenged using these same criteria: professionalism, scientific thoroughness, and prestige.

Generally, since we know that jurors make different kinds of attributions, both with regard to the effectiveness of those setting standards and the culpability of defendants who are and are not in compliance with standards, any strategy using compliance or non-compliance should be tested prior to trial.

Our research has also shown that there are some sex and age differences in the way jurors perceive the significance of compliance. It has been found that women and people over the age of thirty are notably more harsh in their attributions toward corporate defendants than are men and those under thirty. All other things being equal, defense counsel will want to seek out young men as jurors, while the plaintiff would prefer to have older women. People under thirty, in general, are less impressed by either compliance or non-compliance.

By applying attribution theory to the question of the "compliance with standards defense," we have another example of research tending to run counter to the common sense conclusion. Defendants who meet standards for product safety appear to gain far less approval in the minds of jurors than defense lawyers often suppose. When compliance with standards is going to be part of the defense strategy, it is very important that these standards be enhanced and that jurors are persuaded of their legitimacy and reliability.

We have also found that general attitudes toward corporations are not good predictors of how the compliance with standards question will be evaluated. Instead of basing strategy on such general attitudes, it is important to learn about specific attitudes toward specific issues that are going to be raised in the trial.

## § 3-5. Conclusions.

One of the most striking things that emerges from social science research is that jurors are willing to make attributions of blame and cause on the basis of very slight and fragmentary evidence. A number of jurors will use something like co-variation thinking to make attributions of a somewhat complex nature, but the tendency to do so will depend a great deal on the juror's background, education, occupation, and other traits. Many jurors resort quickly to simple, if not naive, "causal schemata," to explain the events they see around them. In making attributions, they can be wrong in what they remember and in what they predict. Selective memory is common, and there is a tendency to disregard fundamental information which should influence attributions.

The importance of previously held attitudes and beliefs has been demonstrated in our investigation into the compliance issue in product liability. Here, the use of attribution theory has enabled us to see that commonly held suppositions about this kind of defense are not nearly so well founded as many have believed. Being able to make use of knowledge about how these attributions will be made is critical when compliance is an issue in a case.

In accident cases, the phenomenon we call defensive attribution may be applicable. Whether or not jurors can be induced to blame the victim will often determine the success of the defense. Insuring that jurors do not blame the victim is a critical task for the plaintiff. Defensive attribution theory can also assist attorneys in identifying jurors who may be oriented toward a verdict for one side or the other.

It is important to recognize, however, that strategies based upon defensive attribution theory must be carefully researched prior to their utilization in a trial. While we have found instances where this concept has been extremely useful, there have been other cases in which strategies based on defensive attribution would have been counter-productive. Where the theory works, it works well.

Only well-designed studies can identify the applicability of the approach for a specific case.

An attorney's ability to make use of what we know about attribution is an invaluable strategic asset in the courtroom. Insights based on attribution theory and research can be used in voir dire and in case presentation. Once research has uncovered the fact that jurors are going to make critical attributions in the trial, it is often possible to base major trial strategy on this finding.

# CHAPTER 4

# THE IDENTIFICATION OF JUROR BIAS



The concept of juror bias is one of the most powerful and important strategic tools behavioral science can offer the trial lawyer. Using a concept of juror bias which is based on juror psychology and, more generally, human behavior studies, social scientists have been able to demonstrate the existence of widespread bias among jurors which goes considerably beyond any legal construction. There are two ways in which this is so.

First, psychologists have discovered ways to show partiality, lack of fairness, and inability on the part of jurors to accept a balanced account of the facts which is not revealed in typical voir dire questions and is unlikely to be acknowledged by jurors themselves.

Second, bias as it is construed by most courts in legal definitions and rulings does not encompass the prejudice and lack of objectivity behavioral science has uncovered. The behavioral science notion of fairness goes well beyond the usual legal notion of fairness and objectivity. The traditional legal perspective which is implemented in typical voir dire questions ignores what we know about human behavior and invites disingenuous responses. Regrettably, the process employed in many courtrooms actually encourages jurors to provide less than forthright answers to voir dire questions.

These are serious assertions, to say the least. In this chapter, we are going to adopt a broader and more complex concept and set of definitions with regard to bias than is usually employed in strategic planning for jury trials. To initiate this topic, we will begin with a short examination of the legal definition of juror bias.

## § 4-1. Legal Definitions of Bias.

The rules governing challenge for cause in the state of California are fairly typical. Challenge for cause will be entertained if:

1. The juror is related to a party in the litigation.
2. The juror has a unique interest in the subject matter.
3. The juror has served on a related case, or the grand jury which indicted the accused.
4. The juror has a state of mind that will prevent her or him from acting with entire impartiality and without prejudice to the rights of either party.

Item 4 is critical. The constitutional guideline is that challenges for cause should be based on "narrowly specified, provable, and legally recognizable bases of partiality." In California, the constitutional standard states that jurors must be possessed of "entire impartiality." In practice, judges have wide latitude in granting challenges for cause.

Their practice can be very uneven and subjective. There is much room for discretion and little hard and fast law.

There are two other areas in which there is law directed at dealing with bias: pretrial publicity and representativeness. Under Chief Justice Warren, the Supreme Court invalidated a number of convictions because of pretrial publicity. In the celebrated case of *Sheppard v. Maxwell,* the murder trial of a prominent physician, the proceedings were called a "Roman Holiday" by the court. It was this "circus-like atmosphere," rather than pretrial publicity per se, which invalidated the outcome in the view of the court.

The Burger court has made this phrase "circus-like atmosphere," rather than a juror's pretrial knowledge of the case, the criterion for reversal.

Whether or not a jury is representative is another way in which the American constitutional system has tried to deal with bias. According to recent court findings, the systematic exclusion of one race, such as Blacks or Hispanics, is unconstitutional. In one case, for example, in which the judge refused during voir dire to ask questions aimed at identifying possible racial prejudice, the conviction was reversed.

While the courts have recognized race as a possible biasing factor, no other demographic trait has been dealt with in similar fashion. There is evidence, however, that women, the young, the elderly, and blue-collar workers, along with Blacks, have been statistically under-represented in jury selection.

## § 4-2. What About the Remedy of Voir Dire?

Apart from issues of representativeness, the fairness issue remains paramount. Voir dire is the only opportunity lawyers have to protect their client against unfair jurors. The fairness issue, from a legal standpoint, has been addressed through peremptory challenges and challenges for cause. Jurors make the first move in this process. If they say they can be impartial, it becomes incumbent upon the litigant who disagrees to prove otherwise. The judge must be convinced that the juror does not know his or her own mind and is not telling the truth when making the claim of impartiality. When the trial is over, a litigant may want to argue on appeal that the jury has not been fair. It is necessary to demonstrate after the fact that the jurors have exhibited "such hostility . . . as to suggest a partiality that could not be set aside." Obviously, this will be a difficult remedy to pursue.

The rules which govern voir dire, as attorneys know, are subject to variation from one court to another. The pattern of questioning permitted may vary. Rules governing the participation of the attorneys themselves will vary from state to state. In Federal Court, judges may permit oral participation by attorneys at their discretion.

Ultimately, the only certain way to deal with a biased juror is through the use of peremptory strikes. Since these are limited, it is doubly important that biased jurors be identified accurately.

So we see that the legal system does recognize bias, using the concepts of fairness and representativeness. The problem with these legal constructions is that they do not go far enough to provide the attorney with what is needed in forming juror selection strategies.

## § 4-3. Bias: The Behavioral Science Definition.

Bias exists when jurors possess intensely held motives or cognitions (values, attitudes, opinions, or beliefs) which inhibit or distort the perception and evaluation of evidence, testimony, or jury instructions. Jurors are also biased if they have arrived at *a priori* verdict conclusions which are intensely held or resistant to change.

## § 4-3(A). Bias Versus Verdict Predisposition.

It is useful to make a distinction between bias on the one hand and verdict predisposition on the other. Bias, as we have seen, is an extreme partiality or lack of fairness. Bias is manifest in the use of stereotyping, the making of extreme attributions, and the tendency to exhibit a certain marked blindness toward incontrovertible facts, the *res gestae* about which both attorneys and the judge are generally in agreement. The claim of behavioral science in this regard is that legal definitions of bias, based on special interest in the matter, or familial relatedness, do not go far enough to embrace these obvious sources of bias.

Verdict predisposition is different from bias. When research demonstrates that certain attitudes and beliefs which jurors hold, or certain experiences they have had, predispose them to favor one side or another, we are dealing with verdict predispositions. We would not argue that verdict predispositions in themselves are a basis for change of venue. The fact that 7 out of 10 prospective jurors show a verdict preference for the plaintiff does not necessarily mean the defendant cannot get a fair trial. It does mean, however, that attorneys should work very hard in voir dire to obtain a jury that is consistent with a verdict preference for the defense.

There is another way of looking at this distinction and that is to use what we can call a "closed mind criterion." Jurors who have a verdict predisposition, or even a stated verdict preference, when acquainted with the case, do not necessarily have a closed mind. They may still be capable of listening with a fair amount of objectivity to arguments for both sides. This is not true of biased jurors. Biased jurors have closed minds. They will screen out arguments for the side which runs against their bias.

## § 4-3(B). A Litigation Sciences Juror Bias Study.

At Litigation Sciences, we have undertaken a number of pretrial experiments and research projects on juror bias and prejudice. In these studies, we have uncovered attitudes, opinions, and beliefs which would have made it virtually impossible for one of the litigants to receive a fair trial. Nevertheless, people holding these cognitions would have been screened as acceptable jurors with a traditionally conducted courtroom voir dire.

The basic notion behind one of our most detailed studies was quite simple. We had listened to voir dire in many judges' courtrooms. We had heard typical judges' voir dire questions, and listened to jurors respond. The emerging picture of bias as it came across in voir dire was very different from the picture we obtained in our research. We therefore decided to design a study that was built around a direct comparison of two alternative approaches for measuring juror bias. The project consisted of more than 3,000 people who were eligible for jury duty in six separate communities in various parts of the country. These were: Philadelphia; Minneapolis/St. Paul; Lincoln, Nebraska; Louisville; Denver; and Seattle.

## § 4-3(C). The Ford Pinto, Tylenol, and MGM Hotel Fire Scenarios.

In the first phase of our study, we used a scenario based on a contrived Ford Pinto product liability case. We divided a large sample of people eligible for jury duty into a Traditional Voir Dire group and a Juror Attitude Survey group. The two groups were matched demographically; the same mix of traits were present in both groups. Using a telephone survey, each group was read the same succinct scenario:

> I would like to ask you about alleged problems with Ford Pinto gas tanks. As you may know, a few years ago there were accidents in which these tanks exploded during rear-end collisions. In one of these accidents a small girl was trapped in the car and burned to death.

Two sets of questions were developed for people who had just finished hearing this scenario: one set for the traditional voir dire group, and one set for the juror attitude survey group.

For the traditional voir dire group, we asked the usual judges' voir dire questions:

> From what you have heard and read, if you were picked to serve on a jury in this case, do you think you could be a fair and impartial juror?
>
> From what you have heard and read, have you formed any judgments about this matter that would make it difficult for the defendant to receive a fair trial?
>
> If you were on the jury in this trial, from what you have seen, heard, and read, do you feel that you could reserve judgment until all the facts were presented?

The answers to these questions can be summarized quickly: sixty-three percent of those questioned said they could be fair and impartial. Fifty-four percent said they had not formed any judgments. Seventy-three percent said they could reserve judgment until all the facts had been presented.

With the Juror Attitude Survey group, we used a different set of questions. We asked prospective jurors if they agreed, disagreed, or didn't know in answer to the following questions:

> Ford was trying to cut corners in safety precautions.
>
> Ford was negligent and careless.
>
> Ford should have to pay money damages for the little girl's pain and suffering.
>
> Ford should have to pay huge damages for its disregard of safety.
>
> Ford and its executives are guilty of murder.

The answers to these questions gave a strikingly different picture of bias. Sixty percent of the respondents in the Juror Attitude Survey group said they believed Ford was cutting corners. Seventy-three percent said Ford was negligent and careless. Seventy-nine percent said Ford should pay damages for pain and suffering. Sixty-four percent said Ford should pay huge amounts for their disregard of safety. Eighteen percent said they believe Ford and its executives are guilty of murder.

## PINTO CASE*

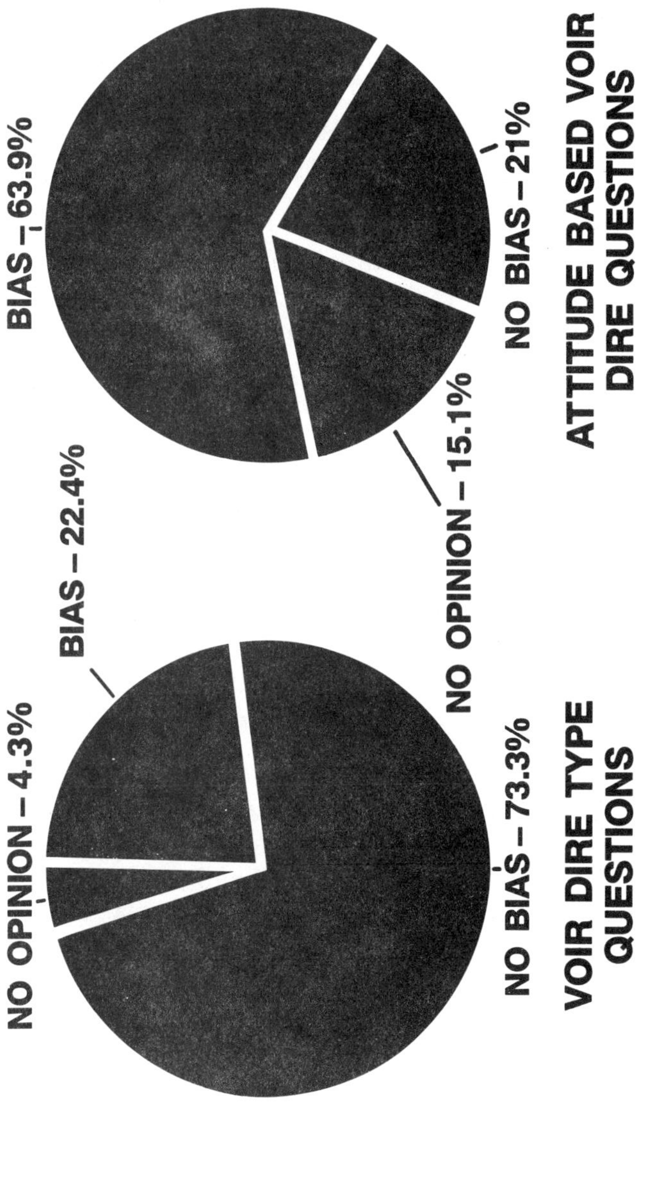


FIGURE 1

*Aggregated data across all questions.

What does all this mean? At the most, about one-third of the potential jurors in the Traditional Voir Dire group questioned admitted to some bias. Yet almost eighty percent in a matched group had already come to the conclusion that Ford should be required to pay money damages, and seventy-three percent said Ford was negligent and careless.

Do jurors lie? Not exactly, but they do not subscribe to the idea of fairness presumed by the court. Since jurors know Ford is guilty, it is not unfair or impartial to think so at the beginning of the trial. When they say they can be fair, they mean it. There is no incompatibility in a juror's mind between finding the defendant guilty and being impartial. For some of them that's what being impartial means.

We revisited these startling results in two criminal examples. The first of these was the case of an alleged Tylenol poisoner. We used this scenario:

> I would like to ask you about a suspect who was apprehended for allegedly inserting poison in Tylenol capsules in Chicago.

We followed with questions to two groups, a Traditional Voir Dire group and a Juror Attitude Survey group, just as in the Pinto case. The same traditional voir dire questions were used as before. These were the questions for the Juror Attitude Survey group:

Do you agree, disagree or hold no opinion —

> The suspect is a criminal.
>
> The suspect is dangerous.
>
> The suspect is beneath contempt.
>
> The suspect must be insane.

The suspect should get a long prison sentence.

The suspect should get the death penalty.

The picture of bias we received in this part of our experiment closely paralleled that in the Ford Pinto case. In answers to judge's traditional voir dire questions, about seventy percent in the Tylenol Voir Dire group said they could be fair and impartial. Over two thirds said they had not formed opinions. Over eighty percent said they could reserve judgment until the facts had been presented.

In the Tylenol Juror Attitude Survey group, almost seventy percent of the respondents said the suspect was a criminal. Seventy percent considered him dangerous. Over sixty percent would give him a long prison sentence. Twenty-two percent would have sentenced him to death.

**TYLENOL CASE***

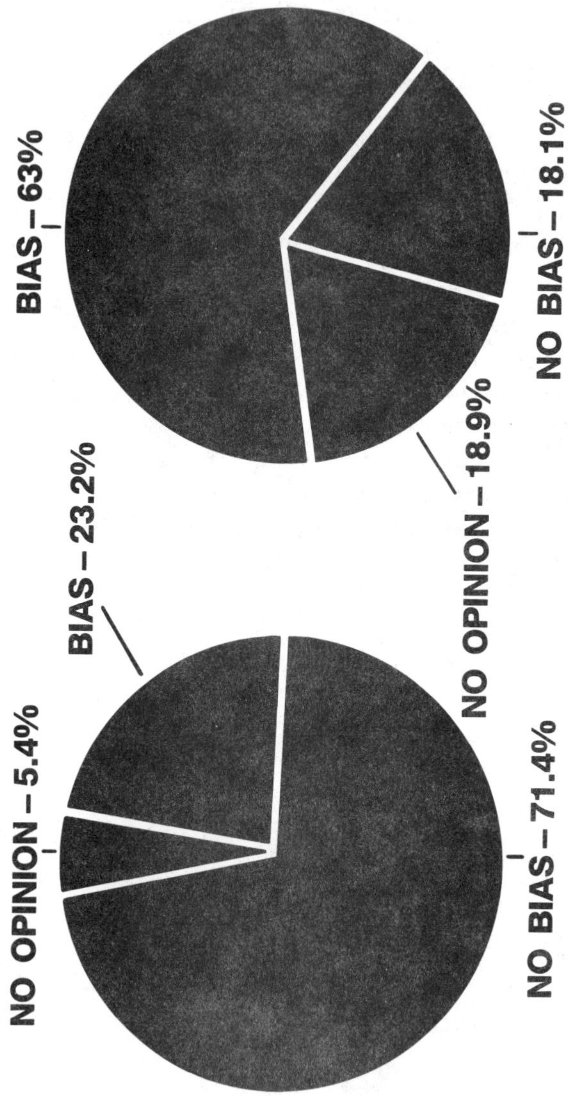


**VOIR DIRE TYPE QUESTIONS**

**ATTITUDE BASED VOIR DIRE QUESTIONS**

**FIGURE 2**

*Aggregated data across all questions.

What do potential jurors mean when they say they can reserve judgment? Obviously, they do not mean that they can wait until they have heard all the evidence before they make up their minds.

Just to be sure, we tested one more case, a fictitious incident involving the MGM hotel fire. We used this scenario:

> I'd like to ask your opinion about a suspect who was apprehended for allegedly starting a fire at a hotel in Las Vegas. A large number of people were killed in this fire. The suspect had been previously convicted in one other felony arson.

We proceeded to ask a Traditional Voir Dire group and a Juror Attitude Survey group the same questions we used in the Tylenol case. The results were nearly identical.

## HOTEL FIRE CASE*

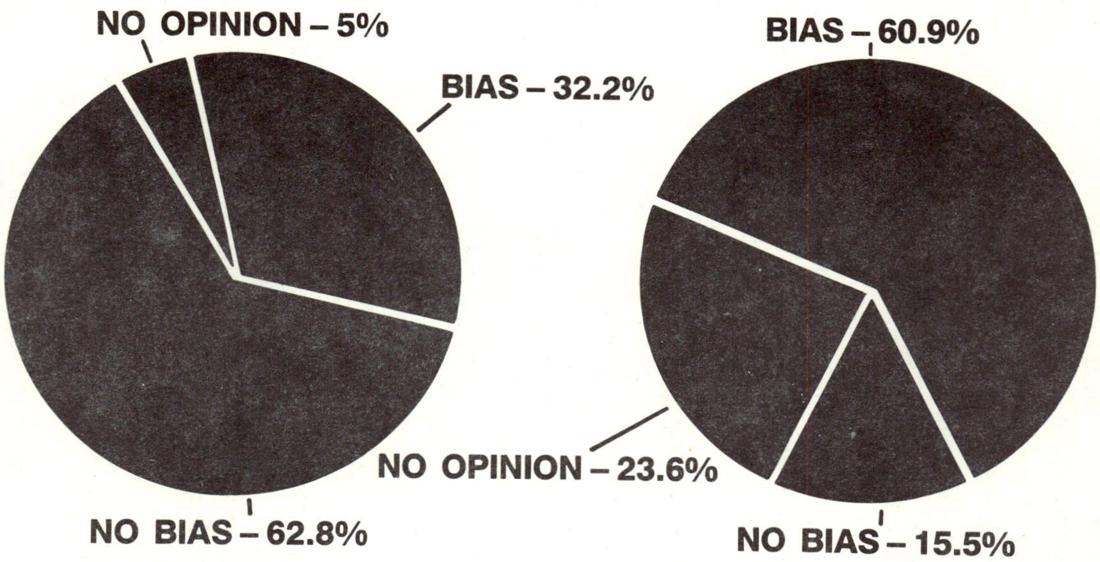


**VOIR DIRE TYPE QUESTIONS**

**ATTITUDE BASED VOIR DIRE QUESTIONS**

**FIGURE 3**

*Aggregated data across all questions.

The lessons to be drawn from our study of over 3,000 people are obvious. First, there is a great deal of juror bias which never gets revealed in traditional voir dire. Second, lawyers must develop strategies for addressing this problem in new and more effective ways.

## § 4-4. Bias: What Are We Looking For?

In a sense, bias is the overriding quality which distinguishes the mind of every human being. All of us carry with us an inventory of values, attitudes, and experiences which we use to organize our perceptions and to make sense out of our world. We tend to have absolute faith in the correctness of these cognitions and rarely challenge their validity. Indeed, most of us react with anger, defensiveness, or confusion when these beliefs are challenged by others. From a psychological perspective, no juror is totally objective about anything; no juror comes into the court with a *tabula rasa.* Everyone has ideas, everyone has attitudes and beliefs, everyone makes attributions of cause and character.

At some point, however, certain jurors will be unable to confront certain basic facts in a case upon which normal men and women agree. These jurors possess some constellation of attitudes and beliefs which make them prejudiced and unable to perceive objective facts. It is extremely important to define when and how this will occur in specific juror candidates.

### § 4-4(A). Revealing Bias.

The single most important strategy in jury trials for defining juror bias is the careful construction of juror profiles. By now, it is well known in the legal community that behavioral science research methods can be used to construct profiles of potential jurors which will reveal verdict preferences. The same techniques can be employed to investigate juror bias.

Through the use of small groups made up of surrogate jurors, it is possible to obtain a general idea of how bias is going to operate in a trial. These surrogate jurors are matched as closely as possible to whom we believe will be actual trial jurors. Bias in these research groups will take a number of forms which can be readily observed. Jurors can give probative value to attitudes they hold about a litigant just as if these had evidentiary standing. They can make vague attributions about a litigant's motivation and character, which will add up to proof of innocence in the juror's mind, or they can display cognitive "blind spots" like those discussed in the preceding paragraph. We frequently see the use of simplistic causal schemata to explain what happened long before jurors have been given very much information about actual events under consideration. Jurors will frequently emphasize certain kinds of evidence which they consider salient, even though the evidence has little importance in the minds of the attorneys or the judge. Jurors can also recall what seem to be trivial bits of information, while other information of considerable legal salience is forgotten.

## § 4-4(B). Stereotyping: The Most Fundamental Category of Bias.

Stereotyping is the most fundamental category of bias. A stereotype is an attitude set. Psychologists noted many years ago the tendency among people to form overall impressions of other people, or objects, on the basis of a relatively small number of traits. Thus, jurors often have attitude sets in place which they use to form overall impressions in this way. Usually, these impressions are negative.

Stereotyped attitude sets, for example, may involve the attribution of negative traits to people simply because they are members of a certain group. Ethnic stereotyping, of course, is one of the best known and most investigated phenomena in American social science.

Jurors invoke stereotypes in response to certain cues. Suppose in a patent case, a chemist is introduced in court as Dr. Ozol, a Turkish immigrant who is a heavily accented scientific research director for a major corporation. If Dr. Ozol is a key witness whose testimony will be critical to the case, we will want to know what kind of stereotypic attitudes jurors might display toward him. We will be particularly interested in attitudes toward credibility and believability which will have the potential of destroying the effectiveness of his testimony. As an obvious example, we would be very dubious about anyone on the jury of Greek or Armenian extraction. Less obvious and more difficult to detect would be those who resent or view with suspicion others who look foreign or speak with an accent.

Stereotypic thinking grows out of the psychological phenomenon called "closure." Closure is one of the ways jurors employ naive causal schemata and make attributions. Closure works very simply. A few pieces of information become available — Turk, corporate employee, immigrant — and the attitude set "closes the design," or "completes the picture." The rest of the traits are filled in.

Through post-trial interviews and many different kinds of psychological research, stereotyping has been exposed as the most fundamental category of bias. When victims of a crime are described as attractive as opposed to unattractive, defendants are sentenced by subjects in studies to longer prison terms. The character and attractiveness of defendants is also a definite factor in decision making among jurors. Studies show that a defendant with an unattractive character will be sentenced to a longer term of incarceration than a more attractive one. One study attached a picture of the defendant to a questionnaire, so that physical appearance became a factor as the study subject considered the facts of the case. Good-looking defendants were judged less harshly than ones who were not good-looking.

Overall, there is clear indication that the characteristics of the litigants in any case will affect the juror's verdict. As the most fundamental type of bias, stereotypes are particularly dangerous. Juror selection strategy must identify them in juror thinking at an early point in our trial preparation. We must learn how stereotypes are going to affect the verdict. Will they determine Psychological Anchors, which are the issues on which jurors decide the case? Will they affect witness credibility? Will they play a significant role in causal attributions? Very likely the answer will be yes to all the above.

### § 4-4(C). Perceptual Biases.

We have been stressing the point that attitudes which are in place in the jurors' minds at the outset of the trial govern the way they perceive what goes on in the courtroom. These attitudes, as well as previous experiences with the kinds of people, objects, and institutions involved in the trial, will all bias perception. As we have seen in our earlier discussions of signal detection and adaptation level, there are abundant opportunities for attitudes and experiences to influence juror perception. These perceptual biases must also be factored into juror selection strategy as well as our case presentation.

### § 4-4(D). Observing Bias in the Courtroom.

We saw earlier in this chapter, when we examined the results of the Litigation Sciences study on juror bias, that traditional voir dire questions do not ferret out the kind of juror bias typically encountered in juror attitude surveys. Why doesn't traditional voir dire uncover more of this underlying bias? One reason for this has to do with situational variables. In all that jurors say and do, they are influenced by the setting they are in, the social context. In any environment where people are exposed to the scrutiny and evaluation of others, they are typically cautious and guarded. Jurors, in the ethos of the courtroom, know that they are supposed to be impartial observers and that their decisions should be fair and unaffected by their own personal preferences, likes or dislikes, or desires for one party to prevail over another.

In this context, jurors cannot be expected to admit their biases. This would be self-condemnatory. Jurors who do admit bias probably do so for one reason. They want to be excused from serving on the jury for the particular trial. At the same time, if they would like to be on the jury, they certainly will not admit that they have opinions and would like to have the opportunity in the jury room to express them. Nor would they admit that their desire to serve is very likely born of bias.

The belief that human beings will freely express their fears and personal disappointments, or their expectations, hopes, and dreams in an open courtroom is an ideal. It is also a myth.

## § 4-5. Juror Bias and Change of Venue Strategy: A Case Example.

Another important application of our knowledge of juror bias is the formulation of arguments in support of change of venue. In making the claim that a litigant cannot receive a fair trial in a particular jurisdiction, it is important to be able to demonstrate widespread and intractable bias among potential jurors in the judicial district. Juror attitude surveys are excellent instruments for establishing that such bias indeed exists. The effectiveness of using a survey in connection with a change of venue argument was seen in a case of complex litigation in the Northwest which followed in the wake of an attempt by the Washington Public Power Supply System (WPPSS) to construct five nuclear power plants in the state of Washington. Construction on two of the plants was stopped, and the project was canceled after the Supply System had spent two and a quarter billion dollars on these plants. This money had been raised through the sale of bonds which were purchased by individual and commercial investors throughout the United States. These bonds were to be paid off, principal and interest, by the 88 public utilities in the Northwest which had entered into contracts with the Supply System. The utilities had planned to set rates they charged their customers at levels high enough to make the payments on these bonds. Subsequently, the Washington State Supreme Court ruled that the utilities' agreements to pay off these bonds was not enforceable.

After the State Supreme Court decision had been rendered, the bond holders brought suit in Federal Court in an attempt to recover their losses. Named as defendants in the suit were the 88 public utilities, the engineering firms which designed and supervised construction, the investment bankers which participated in the sale of the bonds to the public, and Seattle City Light. Litigation Sciences was retained on behalf of the New York investment banker defendants who felt that they could not receive a fair trial in Washington and wanted to file a change of venue motion with the court.

## § 4-5(A). Establishing Exposure and Awareness.

The first task of a change of venue survey is to establish the existence of a widespread awareness of the issues in the trial, that potential jurors recognize who the litigants are, and what activities have gone on in connection with their identity.

In this case, a sample of over 1500 registered voters was undertaken by telephone. It was discovered that virtually all residents of the Western District were aware of WPPSS. In fact, 80 percent of survey respondents were able to recall WPPSS by name on an unaided basis. Derogatory attributions were immediately uncovered. Fifty-eight percent of those surveyed referred to the Supply System as WHOOPS, rather than by its official name and did so without suggestion or aid.

The overall level of name recognition was ninety-eight percent — quite an astounding figure. This was much higher than the recognition level of many public figures and public issues as reported in national polls. Consequently, questions were asked about the amount of media exposure subjects had received. Thirty-five percent of the sample questioned stated that they had seen or heard stories about WPPSS in the media over one hundred times. Fifty-one percent stated that they had heard or seen over fifty stories in the media, and over 68 percent said they had heard or seen over twenty stories.

## § 4-5(B). Establishing the Existence of Self-Interest.

Another objective of a change of venue survey may be to establish whether or not potential jurors perceive a self-interest in the matter. In this case, it was discovered that respondents stated by a ratio of 7-1 that they believed the WPPSS nuclear projects had affected their cost of electricity. Those who believed their cost of electricity had been affected were nearly unanimous in concluding that the effect had been to raise their costs. Clearly, jurors felt a sense of self-interest.

Specific questions about who should bear the loss of the default confirmed the hypothesis that there were pervasive beliefs among potential jurors that the loss should be imposed on parties other than the ratepayers of the defendant utilities. The intensity with which these beliefs were held was virtually uniform for ratepayers and non-ratepayers among survey respondents. By a margin of 7-1, respondents answered that if the loss had to be absorbed by either customer ratepayers or bondholders, then bondholders should suffer the loss. Other confirming measures were obtained. When asked to choose between customer ratepayers and investment bankers, the margin of opinion was more than 11-1 in favor of having the investment bankers who sold the bonds bear the loss. Here again, this belief was held with great intensity.

When the data were analyzed in detail, it was found that opinion in favor of exculpating the ratepayers of the region's utilities was virtually as strong among non-ratepayers as among ratepayers themselves.

The fact that the existence of a strong internal motive, economic self-interest, was well supported with empirical research data added immeasurably to the strength of the change of venue motion. A change of venue was granted.

## § 4-6. Conclusions.

Even jurors who have a conscious awareness of their biases, prejudices, and beliefs will find it difficult to set these pre-existing opinions aside. Such biases will inevitably subconsciously affect the way in which each juror perceives and remembers evidence, testimony, and even the judge's instructions. Jurors will tend to focus on and remember those things which confirm their pre-existing biases, while disregarding contrary evidence. Moreover, when information has been gleaned from a multitude of sources (views of others heard before the trial, media reports, pre-existing personal experiences and beliefs, as well as evidence at the trial itself), this information tends to be integrated into one basic recollection or impression. In the course of forming this overall recollection, jurors will often forget or confuse the source of their information and be unable to clearly distinguish evidence presented in the trial from information they have obtained from other sources.

The basic element of voir dire strategy is that attorneys must have detailed and reliable information about juror biases *before* they conduct voir dire. This information must go far beyond the typical folklore concerning jurors. It must be based on empirical research, and attorneys need to sensitize themselves to the innumerable cues jurors give about their biases in addition to their direct answers to voir dire questions. In addition, attorneys must be prepared to educate judges about juror bias and to develop a climate in the court for more extensive granting of challenges for cause. Finally, until challenges for cause become more widespread and sophisticated in their application, the use of peremptory strikes must be based on hard data, not feelings and intuition.

# CHAPTER 5

# COMMUNICATION STRATEGY: THE PSYCHOLOGY OF PERSUASION



Another domain of behavioral science which can serve as a basis for important trial strategy is the psychology of persuasion. Social psychologists have conducted research into the way in which one person is persuaded by the messages or communications of another. Obviously, this research has import for trial strategy. Under what circumstances is a persuasive communication likely to be enhanced and made more persuasive? Under what circumstances is it likely that the impact of a persuasive communication will be reduced?

One term which is commonly employed when discussing persuasive communications is credibility. A credible message can be defined as one which has persuasive power. A credible message sender, or communicator, is one who is recognized as a reliable source of information, one who can be believed. In this sense, credibility and the ability to persuade are nearly synonymous.

From the first moment jurors encounter an attorney in voir dire, they are evaluating his or her ability to persuade.

They are making decisions about the lawyer's credibility. The advantages which will accrue to an attorney who is able to establish credibility and persuasive power early in the trial will be considerable. By the same token, certain omissions, lack of preparation, or too casual an approach, even during the opening moments of voir dire, can seriously compromise credibility and hamper an attorney in subsequent attempts to be persuasive.

In this chapter we will discuss persuasion strategy. Points made about persuasion are not only applicable to attorneys as communicators; they can also be applied to problems of witness credibility and persuasiveness.

Witnesses often encounter serious problems of credibility. In a recent large antitrust case, for example, an expert economist was testifying about the existence and nature of monopoly power in a relevant sub-market. The defendant had been accused of Sherman Act violations, and the expert witness was someone on whom the plaintiff was counting heavily to make a substantial contribution to the case. Plaintiff's counsel were jubilant after this witness had completed his testimony. They were convinced that this testimony had provided a key element in their case. In fact, they felt that this witness had been so persuasive that he had virtually sold the jurors on their side of the issue.

As part of the work we were doing for the defendant in this case, we had placed a group of surrogate or "shadow" jurors in the courtroom. They had been carefully selected to match the actual jury. Every night, after the trial, these surrogate jurors were interviewed by a communication psychologist. Among other issues investigated, the psychologist asked these jurors specific questions to determine what they thought of plaintiff's expert witness. To our surprise, this witness had not been persuasive, nor had he produced much of an appreciable effect at all. In fact, surrogate jurors viewed him rather negatively. They thought he was condescending. He used arcane and technical vocabulary and, in their view, was trying to talk down to them. In short, he lacked credibility and had not been persuasive.

Why do witnesses fail in this way? The reasons can be complex, but in many instances attorneys lose perspective and do not adequately prepare their witnesses *for jurors.* Trial lawyers normally devote a great deal of time to their witnesses, but they often fail to view witnesses in terms of their possible impact upon jurors from a communications or credibility point of view. On the contrary, lawyers may, in a very short period of time, begin to adopt the communication style of the witness in talking about the subject. Frequently, they pride themselves upon having become experts of a sort on certain technical aspects of the case. Through their interaction, attorney and witness become so familiar with the case, with technical language and vocabulary, and with each other, that a subtle interaction can develop. The lawyer becomes an expert. His sophisticated technical knowledge carries over into the courtroom and can make the witness's testimony incomprehensible to many jurors.

Thus, it is easy for attorneys to overlook the fact that witnesses, first and foremost, must communicate effectively with jurors. The power to persuade and convince jurors, using certain technical information, resides in the witness's ability to make this information credible and comprehensible.

Obviously, the matter of persuasion and credibility is of paramount importance from the earliest stages of trial preparation. It is another area in which communication and social psychology theory can combine to yield important strategic ideas. Social psychology approaches the matter of persuasion by using a basic model of communication. We will briefly examine this model. In the course of doing so, it will be evident that such a model can help explain, from a behavioral standpoint, much of what goes on in a jury trial.

## § 5-1. A Basic Model of Communication.

The basic model employed by communication psychologists when conducting research into persuasion and credibility employs five terms to define the essential elements of any communication. These elements relate to the sender, the receiver, the message, the channel of the communication, and feedback.

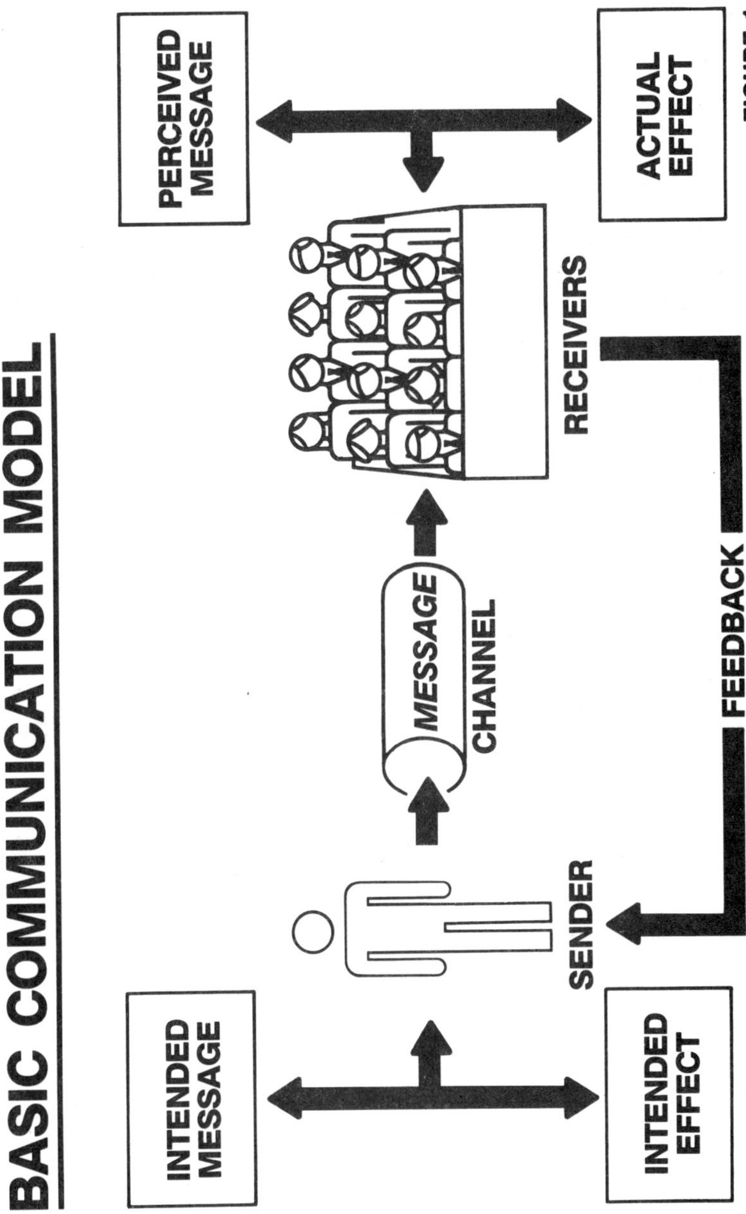
BASIC COMMUNICATION MODEL
INTENDED MESSAGE
INTENDED EFFECT
SENDER
MESSAGE
CHANNEL
RECEIVERS
FEEDBACK
PERCEIVED MESSAGE
ACTUAL EFFECT

FIGURE 1

*The Sender.* The sender in any act of communication is the source of the communication. The sender has both an intended content and an intended effect for the message directed at the judge, jury or some audience outside the courtroom. The communication process begins with the action of a sender.

*The Message.* In the courtroom, messages must frequently occur in the form of verbal or written language. The words and symbols used in the message must be oriented as closely as possible to the background, interests, needs and predispositions of the receivers of the message. Otherwise, the effect may be a failure to capture the jury's attention or achieve comprehension.

*The Receivers.* The receiver is the person, group, or object whose act of reception completes the communication. Effective communication can occur only when the content of the message processed by the receiver closely corresponds to that which was transmitted. Because of the common phenomena of selective attention, comprehension, and retention, any attempt to communicate without regard to the receiver's motivational influences is doomed to failure unless the communicator has phenomenal luck.

*The Channel.* The medium through which the message is sent in the courtroom is most frequently the spoken word, although various forms of nonverbal communication are important as well. These include body movement and paralanguage (voice qualities and non-language sounds such as yawning, sighs of exasperation, groaning, etc.). Other nonverbal factors such as dress and cosmetics also affect communication. Attorneys have employed the use of blackboards, flip charts, and large exhibit boards as communication channel media for many years. Recently, electronic technology has extended communication channel opportunities to include computerized image presentation and video communication.

*Feedback.* Some verbal or nonverbal feedback is essential for any effective communication effort. If the sender perceives that the intended message has not produced the intended effect, the sender can modify the message and try again. Thus, feedback makes face-to-face interpersonal communication highly efficient. In the courtroom, however, effective feedback is frequently difficult because the attorney and his intended audience are physically separated. Hence, a smile, an affirmative nod, a frown, or some other type of response may represent the extent of available feedback.

This model has a number of analytic advantages. By isolating the various elements in the communication, it is possible to conduct research and make statements about the process of communication in a clear and unambiguous manner. By making clear the separation of the message from the channel, it is possible to analyze the content of the message apart from the impact of the medium through which it travels. By making clear the separation in the process of the sender and the receiver, we can raise questions about whether or not the message sent and the message received are the same. We have already seen the value of doing this in the case of visual exhibit strategy.

Because so much of the communication that occurs in the courtroom is verbal, our focus here will be limited to spoken messages. In other words, the channel or medium will be human speech. Obviously, another medium which is often used in jury trials is the medium of visual communication as was discussed in Chapter 2.

An attorney's role as a message sender is something that can be studied and evaluated. The attorney's task is to conceive the message and then encode it. Encoding is the term employed by communication psychologists to designate the procedure through which the message, as conceptualized, is put into a form appropriate to the channel through which it will be sent. In the case of a verbal message, encoding is a process of choosing certain words which will be spoken to jurors. This is extremely important. It will be seen that the choice of words, or the way in which a message is encoded, will often have a great deal to do with how effective that message will be. It has already been demonstrated that the encoding procedures used in the formulation of visual messages can be very important. This is also true of verbal messages. At the lowest level of intellectual abstraction, words paint pictures for people. In a courtroom context, it is critically important that the attorney clearly understand the word driven visual images he is sending to jurors.

The social sciences can contribute in many ways to making an attorney more effective in the role of message sender. This role begins with how the message is conceptualized. The opening chapters of this book have emphasized how important it is to conceptualize an attorney's message in terms of juror attitudes and opinions, as well as juror tendencies to make attributions. Once a message has been conceptualized, it is also important to make certain that it is effectively encoded. Suppose, for example, that our pretrial research has indicated that several Psychological Anchors, or attitudinal issues, are going to be very important in this trial. It will be necessary to carefully choose the precise language to be employed in presenting these Anchors to a jury. This is what is meant by encoding the message.

Jurors, in this communication model, are the receivers of the message. Their task is to decode the message and conceptualize what the message means. In the case of an effective message, their conceptualization will be the same as the one that the attorney intended to send. Both sender and receiver will have the same understanding of what has been said. It is possible, of course, that jurors may understand the message but fail to be persuaded by it. It can be maintained, however, that barring some gratuitous outcome, understanding the message will be a necessary prerequisite to being convinced by it.

It is important for attorneys to be aware of the power they exercise as message senders. Like the pitcher in baseball or the server in tennis, play begins with their actions. They are in a position to exercise more control over the outcome of the communication process than the juror/receiver. They "put the ball in play" so to speak. They have it in their power to refine and test their conceptualization of the message. Using research methods, lawyers can learn how jurors are likely to function as message receivers and how they are likely to perform the task of decoding the messages they receive.

## § 5-2. Strategic Approaches to Sender Credibility and Persuasiveness.

To what extent is a message persuasive because of the impact or impression made by its sender? Communication psychologists have isolated a number of important factors in sender credibility. These include expertise or competence, trustworthiness, dynamism or likability, and similarity or the ability to induce affiliation.

Expertise or competence can be perceived by a jury when they evaluate a witness or an attorney's manner of delivery and knowledge of the subject. A smooth, assured delivery, with the proper amount of eye contact, good diction, rounded sentence structure, and so forth, will be interpreted as a sign of competence. A command of the subject is also very important in conveying the impression that one is an expert. Groping of any kind, signs of disorganization, or possessing incomplete information, missing parts of which have to be obtained or looked up at another time, are all signs that jurors will interpret as incompetence or lack of expertise.

Trustworthiness is a second important sender credibility factor. Trustworthiness is closely related to a jury's conviction that an attorney or witness will only speak the truth and make assertions based on valid information. When jurors suspect that the source of the communication is being insincere or making statements that he himself only partially believes, the attorney or witness is compromised as a trustworthy source. This is why exposing the patent untruth of something an opposing attorney has said, sometimes without even being aware that he was misinformed, can be a powerful courtroom tactic. Once trustworthiness has been lost in court, it can very rarely be regained. Related to trustworthiness is what some experts refer to as the safety factor. Jurors can be said to feel safe with someone when he or she is perceived to be honest and well-intentioned. The safety to which we refer in this context is mainly a matter of feeling that it is safe to believe what the attorney or witness says and that there is no "risk" in doing so.

Dynamism is also an important factor in sender credibility. An enthusiastic communicator will be more convincing than a lackluster, low-key one. This can be taken too far, however. Jurors will recognize over-ebulliance and tend to distrust it. Studies have also shown that a communicator who is liked will be more persuasive than one who is not liked or toward whom feelings are neutral. Whenever jurors can be made to feel affiliation or liking toward the communicator, there will be enhanced credibility. Such feelings can often follow from a sense of similarity with the attorney or witness, based on common values and supposed common background. Feelings of affiliation can sometimes also be established by a sense of co-orientation. That is, the feeling that the message sender and jurors are coming at matters from the same perspective or the feeling that this person is "one of us." Various rhetorical devices can be employed to create such feelings of similarity and co-orientation.

## § 5-3. Jurors as Message Receivers: Affective Versus Cognitive.

Jurors are message receivers and information processors. The messages they receive and the information they process become the basis for their decisions. Through conducting extensive pretrial and post-trial research, it has been discovered that jurors can be classified into a dichotomy based on their decision-making style. By decision-making style, communication psychologists refer to the way in which jurors decode information, what information they are willing to decode, and how they will use this information in making decisions. The basic dichotomy or two-fold distinction into which jurors can be placed is the dichotomy of affective versus cognitive thinkers. It is important to emphasize that this distinction focuses on decision style and not intelligence. Bright and dull people are found in each category.

From a lawyer's perspective, an affective juror is one who makes decisions on an emotional rather than a rational basis. Affective jurors are impulsive decision-makers. They often base their decisions on highly selective perception and organization of what they see and hear, rather than reserving judgment until all the facts have been gathered. They are not information seekers because they are not information processors. When information is presented to them, they are inclined to reformulate and shape it until it fits their previously held world view or set of conclusions based on how they feel about the matter. These jurors tend to be responsive to what the particular parties in the litigation symbolize, for example, "big business" and "the little man." Consequently, they are heavily swayed by the images an attorney may create of the parties involved. This is especially the case if the parties are portrayed in stereotypic terms that are consistent with the affective juror's preconceived notions. Affective thinkers are people who come to conclusions without making much of an effort to sift the evidence, review the facts, or critically analyze the subtleties of witness testimony.

Who are the people most likely to be affective jurors? Research has shown that affective jurors are more likely to be women than men. They are more often deeply devoted to religious principles or philosophies of life. Affective jurors are often members of minority groups. They are typically not college educated, but if they are, they have generally majored in the arts or humanities rather than in one of the physical sciences. Affective jurors tend to dislike numerical concepts and abstractions. They tend to be creative and may be "artsy-craftsy." These people are the poets of the world; people who frequently conduct their lives on the basis of how they "feel," what they believe, and what "ought to be." In a debate or argument, an affective decision-maker might say, "Don't tell me that, I don't want to hear it!"

Cognitive jurors, on the other hand, are usually very orderly and logical decision-makers. They are information seekers because they are information processors. Cognitive thinkers balance their checkbooks, organize their lives (as well as the lives of others), and are generally intellectually fastidious and controlled. They are the kind of people who can always find the warranty to their five-year-old lawnmower because they inevitably have a file marked "lawnmower warranty." Jurors who are cognitive thinkers make "to do" lists and methodically do everything on the list. Affective thinkers, on the other hand, make such lists with the best of intentions and inevitably lose the lists.

Cognitive thinkers have an intrinsic curiosity and, hence, will seek out facts and information. They are stereotypic inductive problem solvers. Cognitive jurors are often young MBA's or people who have majored in mathematics, drafting, bookkeeping, accounting, engineering, or one of the physical sciences in college. They tend to be intellectually rigorous, logical, and usually less empathetic than their affective counterparts.

It is important for lawyers to understand this affective/cognitive distinction. First of all, many lawyers are cognitive thinkers and generally anticipate that others will be so as well. As cognitive thinkers, lawyers not only view their case in "logical" cognitive terms but also construct their arguments and encode their messages from a cognitive perspective. When jurors fail to respond appropriately or render verdicts "inconsistent with the evidence," attorneys frequently assail jurors as stupid, inept, or incapable of dealing with complex or sophisticated issues. In many cases, the problem resides not so much with jurors but rather with lawyers who fail to make their communication consistent with the characteristics of the message receivers. In the vast majority of cases, jurors diligently attempt to do a good job. In too many cases, lawyers frustrate or inhibit the ability of jurors to do so.

Another reason why the affective/cognitive dichotomy is important relates to the design and structure of intended messages for the jury. If the lawyer is confronted with cognitive jurors, the information, testimony, and lawyer arguments should be consistent with this decision-making style. If on the other hand, the jury is composed of affective jurors, communications should be constructed to reflect this orientation. What course of action should be pursued if the jury represents a mixture of both kinds of jurors? Fortunately, there is an easy answer to this dilemma. Affective jurors will require affective structures and affective arguments. Even though cognitive jurors will not particularly like an affective approach, they typically possess the rigor to place a cognitive structure on affective arguments. Hence, the decision rule is to attend to the affective jurors; cognitive jurors will be able to attend to themselves!

In the many trials that Litigation Sciences has observed, it is interesting to note that successful plaintiff lawyers are frequently masters at structuring affective communications. At the same time, most defense lawyers adhere to a highly structured cognitive approach.

## § 5-4. Strategic Approaches to Message Credibility and Persuasiveness.

A persuasive communication is a communication aimed at influencing attitudes and beliefs. It may have the objective of changing pre-existing beliefs and attitudes or reinforcing attitudes which are in place. Persuasive messages may also be directed at bringing about some action or change in behavior. The messages delivered in an attorney's case presentation serve all of the above objectives at one time or another. Ultimately, these messages are directed at bringing about a specific juror action, the rendering of a particular verdict.

Communication psychologists have studied the question of the content of a persuasive communication. Among the questions which have been investigated are the way in which such a message should be organized, the order of arguments, the advantages and disadvantages of using certain kinds of content, as well as certain general factors in the communication which make it more or less effective. One basic characteristic we would expect to find in a persuasive communication is a conclusion which follows from the facts in the case. This is elementary but can be overlooked. Moreover, the conclusion must follow from the facts *as far as the jurors are concerned.* When it is clear that some conclusion is based on facts which are made explicit, most jurors will try to decide whether or not they believe these facts. They will then decide if the conclusion follows from these facts.

Why do jurors ignore facts after an attorney has told them these facts are important and that his case rests upon their truth? The answer is quite simple. Jurors do not always choose to regard matters the way attorneys do. They may have attitudes and beliefs in place which render them unable to accept certain facts or to avoid these facts altogether and come at the case from an entirely different perspective, a perspective of which the attorney may not be aware.

Trial attorneys are generally excellent communicators. They usually do not make the error of presenting facts which fail to support the conclusion they wish to draw. When their messages have credibility problems, it is generally because the facts on which their arguments are based are rejected. They suffer a defeat in the case because they are arguing from premises which are simply not acceptable to the jury from an attitudinal standpoint.

Research has demonstrated that jurors frequently make end runs around technical arguments. This is particularly true of affective thinkers. They may even decide that the whole argument advanced by an attorney, the whole passel of facts and conclusions, is simply not a part of what should be considered. These jurors may be stubborn, but they are not imperceptive or unintelligent. At the end of the trial, they may not even remember the attorney's argument, at least not until their minds are jogged. This is because they have been off on a completely different line of reasoning on their own, with its own "facts" and conclusions.

Thus, the question of making arguments logical from the lawyer's perspective is not an easy one to resolve. Most jurors will expect logic in a trial presentation; but the denial of emotional factors may compromise credibility in cases where there is an obvious emotional component. This is particularly true in cases where severe, if not tragic, personal consequences have formed the basis of plaintiff's claim. Once again, planning strategy with respect to the use of an emotional argument will depend in part upon what can be learned in pretrial research about jurors' decision-making styles and the presence on the jury of affective or cognitive thinkers.

Emotional appeals can be of two basic kinds. One kind of emotional appeal is one in which the message is accompanied by a positive emotional context. The communicator may attempt to convey good feelings or arouse positive feelings in the audience. On the other hand, many persuasive messages are delivered in a negative emotional context. Foremost among these are messages which in some way constitute fear appeals or attempts to frighten the receiver of the message into some kind of action or attitude change.

## § 5-4(A). The Strategic Use of Emotional Messages.

Messages which contain positive emotional content can often prove useful in court. Whenever an attorney can do something which will make jurors feel good, an advantage will probably be created. Of course, this must stop short of something that jurors recognize as frivolous, or an attempt to be ingratiating. Humor is the most obvious way to cloak a persuasive message with positive feelings. Interesting anecdotes or story elements can add interest to an attorney's presentation. Reassuring jurors that they are doing their work well and attentively, or that they will be able to cope with something coming up in the trial that will make special demands upon them, may also be useful. Serving on a jury in a long trial can be tedious. Providing small moments of pleasant relief for jurors will help win their allegiance.

Obviously, making a communication easy to listen to and easy to understand and remember is a most basic and important way to make jurors feel positive about what they are hearing.

The second type of emotional appeal is one which tries to persuade through the use of some kind of fear appeal or anxiety-provoking element in the message. There are many opportunities in the course of conducting jury trials for using a fear appeal of some kind to try to influence jurors. Fear appeals are the most common kind of emotional argument and are quite familiar. Politicians often threaten the electorate with some harrowing consequences if their policies are not supported. Advertisers threaten dire problems in health and hygiene if their products are not used. Fear appeals are commonplace from the pulpit. Messages from service organizations against drunk drivers depict a body covered with a sheet lying alongside a smashed car. An anti-smoking commercial depicts the ugly inside of a diseased lung.

Do people actually change their attitudes and behavior in response to this kind of appeal? How well advised is an attorney in a personal injury case, for example, to try to scare the jury into identifying with his client's suffering? Research into fear appeals or "anxiety-provoking stimuli," as they have been called, has produced mixed results. One study on the use of fear appeals to promote dental hygiene reported some success in shifting attitudes in the direction of better dental hygiene. Yet another study produced somewhat the opposite results.

Fear appeals will be successful persuasive devices when they are quite strong, when the premises of the fear appeal are believed by the recipient, and when the recipients believe that the recommended procedures for avoiding the dangers illustrated in the appeal do in fact work.

This can be applied to a common situation found in litigation in which a fear appeal might be appropriate. Suppose the plaintiff is a quadriplegic and claims his condition is the result of a defective automobile. Very large monetary damages are being requested. To successfully employ a fear appeal strategy, experienced plaintiff counsel recognize that the fear appeal must be strong, unrelenting and unambiguous. In addition to graphic details of plaintiff's past, present, and future suffering, the jury must be provided with unpleasant, frightening, or anxiety-provoking associations to make the fear appeal credible.

In a case alleging a design defect in automobile tires, jurors were shown various color photographs of the plaintiff lying in a hospital bed with surgical skull tongs implanted in his head. After seeing the pictures, the jurors were then presented with an actual skull tong as an exhibit. The tongs were passed from one juror to the next as they listened to a neurosurgeon describe the implantation procedure as equivalent to medieval torture. Later in the same trial, jurors were shown video tapes of tires literally disintegrating and flying apart at high speed. Post-trial interviews with jurors confirmed that plaintiff's counsel had indeed developed a sense of frightening association with the defendant's product.

The use of fear appeals must be undertaken with caution. Studies have demonstrated that if the fear inducing stimuli are too extreme, people will selectively reject the anxiety provoking mechanism as a form of psychological self protection. Plaintiff lawyers frequently fall into this trap with "Day In The Life Of" video tape presentations.

Over exposing the jury with gruesome or heart-rending depictions of plaintiff's condition may well cause jurors to avoid thinking about the plaintiff or to even discuss his condition with others during deliberations.

When using fear appeals, it is very important that the jurors believe the remedy sought will ameliorate the conditions depicted in the fear appeal. If the jurors think, even subconsciously, that "all the money in the world is not going to help this poor plaintiff," they will be inclined to limit the monetary award. If, however, jurors accept the suggestion that by returning a large verdict, the message sent to the manufacturer might help reduce or eliminate the conditions that led to the production of a defective product (and the horrible consequences to the plaintiff in this particular case), they are very likely to award substantial punitive damages.

## § 5-4(B). Rhetorical Questions.

Studies have demonstrated that if people are not intensely involved in a topic of discussion, rhetorical questions will tend to make them pay closer attention to what they are hearing. This would suggest, however, that when jurors are paying close attention and are quite intensely involved with the subject matter, the use of rhetorical questions will do little to enhance communication effectiveness. At other times in the trial, when jurors are not attentive and are less involved, rhetorical questions can be an excellent device to arouse and recapture attention.

When arguments are not particularly strong or convincing, rhetorical questions can have the effect of calling attention to the weakness of the argument. This means, among other things, that if the attorney is not careful, the use of rhetorical questions in this situation can be counterproductive. At the same time, using rhetorical questions to call attention to weaknesses in an opposing argument can be an excellent communication strategy.

Of course, since rhetorical questions are likely to be viewed as argumentative, they will have to be used sparingly in the opening statement. When employed carefully and at certain key junctures, they can make a definite positive impact.

### § 5-4(C). Strategy in Organizing the Content of a Communication.

One of the most compelling questions in the organization of a persuasive communication is whether the argument should be one-sided or two-sided. The relative effectiveness of one-sided versus two-sided communications has been investigated by researchers in communication, and there is some reason to believe that an argument which presents only one side of an issue will be recognized as containing an obvious bias. Whenever a one-sided argument is presented, it will be possible to weave in counter-arguments. These arguments can be left unchallenged, or they can, in the course of the communication, be refuted.

In general, one-sided communications seem to be far more effective when the group hearing the communication is initially favorably disposed to the point of view being espoused. One-sided communications are also most effective in strengthening a pre-existing belief. Where there is no initial agreement between sender and receiver, however, a communication which presents both points of view can often be more effective in bringing about a change in conviction than one which contains only one point of view.

Use of one-sided versus two-sided arguments in jury trials can comprise a subtle strategic dilemma. Deciding between these two approaches will require knowledge of who the jurors are and a sophisticated appreciation of the strength of one's position going into the trial. Credibility is the ultimate criterion.

First, consider the example of a case in which there are many good arguments which can be put forward on behalf of both sides. Suppose, further, that pretrial juror research has revealed a good deal of support among jurors for both the plaintiff and the defendant and that many potential jurors face the dilemma of feeling there are identifiable strengths on both sides. Let us suppose further that the jurors who are actually chosen to serve in the trial are cognitively-oriented, that is, they are people who are going to be active information processors in the trial and make a decision on a largely factual basis. They are people who like to think with a certain amount of "logical" rigor and base their decisions on the facts as the lawyers know them.

Given the above kind of situation, an attorney who completely ignores the position of the other side will risk losing credibility. There is good reason to suppose that in such a case the most credible approach will be one in which the arguments for the other side are presented and ultimately transcended or refuted by an appeal to a more reasonable, more just, and better-grounded set of counter arguments. To pretend that the position of the other side does not exist, or have any validity whatsoever, risks being censured by jurors who themselves acknowledge that there is a certain amount of strength on both sides and who believe that the arguments for both sides are worth taking seriously.

If we change the scenario slightly, specifying that the actual jurors chosen for the trial are more inclined to be affective thinkers, our strategy might be a little different. As we have seen, jurors who are affective thinkers tend to make decisions more on the basis of feelings than "logical" thought. They tend to go with their "gut feelings" when making decisions. With such a jury, there will probably be less of a credibility problem if only one side of an argument is presented. In fact, presenting counter-arguments and their refutation to such a jury may be confusing.

Of course, strategy will have to take into account whether or not we are coming at matters from the side of the defendant or the plaintiff. As we shall see in the next chapter, one of the most important occasions on which to decide whether or not to use a two-sided argument is the opening statement. When the defense is giving their opening statement, the jury will already have heard the plaintiff's arguments. If defense counsel proceeds to present the defense case with no reference to the plaintiff's position, he or she may experience a problem of credibility. From the plaintiff's point of view, it will sometimes be good strategy to present a two-sided argument which anticipates and refutes the defense opening statement. This technique, called inoculation, is based on the idea that opposing arguments will be heard by jurors, or occur to them, sooner or later and that there is advantage to be gained by having jurors hear these arguments in the context of their refutation. We will come back to the technique of inoculation in the context of voir dire later in this book.

In situations where pretrial research reveals that the case for one side is much more convincing to jurors than the case for the other, lawyers for the side which rates highly among potential jurors should not raise counter-arguments. When dealing from a position of great strength, an attorney will probably appear most credible by sticking to a basically one-sided presentation. Certainly raising and refuting arguments from the other side that jurors are not inclined to take seriously would compromise credibility.

When a careful analysis of the case has been undertaken and juror predispositions dictate that a two-sided argument will be useful, there is a proper method for formulating such an argument. This method is based on the use of primacy and recency effects. That is, the tendency to remember those parts of an argument which come first and those parts of an argument which come last. These effects dictate that it is best to begin with a strong presentation of the pro point of view. Given that a two-sided message strategy was selected, it is anticipated that there will be some resistance to this initial presentation. In order to enhance credibility and to support the initial arguments, the attorney next demonstrates a knowledge of the best arguments which will come from the other side and refutes these in the most effective way possible. Finally, the argument concludes with a forceful restatement of the initial pro position.

## § 5-5. Witness Strategy: Another Message Sender.

Experienced trial attorneys are always concerned about the impact of their witnesses. In the recently concluded criminal trial of automobile manufacturer John Z. DeLorean, a government witness was supposed to have been the key to the prosecution of the case. Unfortunately for the government, the jury did not believe this witness. In fact, his lack of credibility was a critical element in the defendant's acquittal.

In trial after trial, one can point to examples of witness testimony which seems to contain relevant and persuasive evidence but which is nevertheless undermined because of the witness's low personal credibility. At Litigation Sciences, we have often had the experience of hearing jurors admit after a trial that what the witness had to say had an important potential bearing on the case, but that it was discounted because of a lack of credibility. This matter is of such importance that we have sought out the determinants of witness credibility.

Witness credibility is predicated on three qualities. The first of these is expertise in the area in which the witness is testifying. Second, the effectiveness of the witness's message depends in part on the belief of the receivers that the witness has attitudes and beliefs similar to their own. Third, the witness must evince a lack of bias toward either party. Based on these three qualities, witnesses can be evaluated in order to predict how jurors will perceive their credibility.

Expertise in the area of testimony is the easiest to evaluate. For most juries, it tends to be something which is both social and pragmatic. It is often related to higher education and formal credentials, but it may also be related to the witness's experience and whether or not the witness is "in a position to know." Under most circumstances, testimony about the safety of a drug from a local pharmacist will not be very credible. However, a research chemist for the FDA might be "in a position to know" even though he may have had little or no direct experience with the drug. In an airline disaster case, a member of the FAA might have credibility on the grounds of expertise, despite a lack of formal education in the field of aeronautical engineering.

How jurors will rank the importance of formal credentials vis-à-vis practical experience, or being in the right place to have gained critical knowledge, will be a function of the jurors' own educational background and personal experience. Lawyers rarely have problems establishing the requisite level of witness expertise for most jurors.

The perception that a witness possesses a shared cultural identity with jurors is referred to as co-orientation. In a recent product liability case, the plaintiff brought in a witness at great expense to testify about the alleged metallurgical defects in a product. Defendant's counter testimony came from an engineer who had lived and worked for many years in the same community from which the jurors were drawn. When interviewed after the trial, it was difficult for the jurors to articulate the precise reasons why they found the credibility of the local engineer impeccable but were dubious about the plaintiff's witness. When we probed further, we discovered that jurors had taken a jaundiced view of the plaintiff's witness because he had been brought in from a foreign country. They were also put off by his accent and the fact that he appeared slightly bored with the proceedings.

In the case of the foreign expert, we see our second criterion for credibility at work — co-orientation or similarity. Psychologists use the term "co-orientation" to describe the relationship jurors see between themselves and another person they think holds similar values, beliefs, attitudes, and life experiences. In the case of the local engineer in the above example, co-orientation was imputed to the witness on the basis of his local identity. In another recent case, an expert identified with a local university was perceived to be more credible than another internationally recognized expert with a more impressive background but with no local identity. Frequently a professor from the local state university will have greater jury appeal than a leading expert in the same field from a more prominent or prestigious institution located in another part of the country.

The third element to be noted as a criterion for credibility is bias. The extent to which the witness has a perceived commitment to one side or the other will have a bearing on credibility. As an example, testimony from corporate personnel may be discounted by jurors because of the attribution of personal vested interest. Even though jurors are very sensitive to this issue, many corporate defendants tend to rely upon their own in-house technical experts rather than retaining independent, outside experts. While technical experts from the company may, in fact, be the world's leading authorities on some subject, their credibility is normally an issue with jurors. In post-trial interviews, jurors have expressed skepticism concerning the capacity of company witnesses to be truly independent, impartial, and free of bias. Indeed, many company witnesses have confessed to our staff concerns regarding the impact of their performance as a witness on their careers.

Thus, the basic juror strategy for the use of witnesses is to carefully insure their credibility. Aside from the obvious characteristics that we all like in other people, the witness must have recognized expertise, there must be a perceived high degree of co-orientation between the witness and the jurors, and the jurors must be convinced that the witness is not committed to any specific outcome in the trial.

## § 5-5(A). Strategies to Enhance Credibility.

One way to enhance the credibility of witnesses is to employ the distinction we have made between cognitive and affective jurors. Cognitive jurors will respond most favorably to witnesses who are logical and straightforward in their testimony and who present facts in a detailed, structured, and logical manner. Supporting this testimony with charts, graphs, and technical exhibits is very desirable. When it is necessary to present technical testimony to jurors who are affectively oriented, it is helpful to employ concrete examples and analogies which will be familiar to jurors. Presenting technical data in an abstract form will normally be counterproductive.

Order of presentation can also be employed to make witnesses more effective. Witnesses placed first and last will be better remembered than those in the middle. Since jurors are more likely to be inattentive during long periods of protracted witness testimony, it is important to place the most important witnesses, and the most appealing and articulate, first or at the very end of a series of witnesses.

Sometimes our selectivity of witnesses will be limited. There may only be a single witness who can supply an important piece of the evidentiary puzzle. When this is the case, we must go with whom we have. We must manage the impact of this witness's credibility, whatever it might be. One of the ways we can do this is by taking advantage of the "sleeper effect."

The sleeper effect refers to the increase or decrease in the credibility of a message, or the amount of belief induced by the message, which occurs after a lapse of time. Such a delayed effect is directly related to the credibility of the source of the communication. By positioning the witness either early or late in the trial, it is possible to exercise some influence over the impact made by the witness's personal credibility.

There are many examples of the sleeper effect in everyday life. Advertisers often depend upon this phenomenon to realize benefits from their expenditures. Their audience may not believe claims about an advertised product when they first see and hear a televised advertisement. Two weeks later, however, they may purchase the product because they remember its alleged benefits without recalling the original source of their information. As an example, many television viewers may dislike the Charmin bathroom tissue ads but actually purchase the product because it is the brand name recognized on the supermarket shelf at the time of purchase. Recall of the specific ad has probably dissipated at that particular moment in time. The consumer remembers the product and its benefits without remembering the source of the information.

The sleeper effect may also occur because the message is disassociated from a source of questionable credibility. This has strategic implications for trial attorneys. In the case of a witness with low credibility, testimony may be viewed more favorably by jurors after a lapse of some days or weeks, than immediately following the witness's appearance on the stand. Thus, when a witness of questionable credibility must be used, that witness should be questioned early in the trial. With this approach, jurors will have time to separate the message from a source they may consider dubious.

What if we have a high credibility witness? In this case, it is desirable that jurors continually associate the message with the source. If we use a high credibility witness early in the proceedings, his effectiveness will be reduced. Valuable and important expert witnesses may lose much of their impact if a substantial period of time lapses between their testimony and the jury's deliberation.

Sometimes our hand is forced in the positioning of a witness, and our high credibility witness must testify at the beginning of the trial. In this case, it may be possible to overcome the sleeper effect. One way to do this is to make sure there is as much repetition as possible in the witness's direct testimony. Research on persuasion indicates that repetition is useful in two situations. The first is when a message is hard to understand. The second is when it is necessary to maintain opinion change when there is a lapse of time between the presentation of the message and the listener's decision, reaction or overt behavior. Continual references back to the witness's testimony throughout the trial will be extremely helpful in this situation as well.

There is also a possible defensive strategy in regard to the sleeper effect. Suppose our opponent has used a low credibility witness early who delivered a somewhat believable message. In this situation, the concern is that jurors will only remember the message and forget their reservations about the witness. Throughout the remainder of the trial, we can refer to this witness explicitly, causing jurors to renew the association in their minds between the message and its source. Thus, our strategy with regard to witness testimony is to remind jurors of the identity of our own high credibility witnesses and of our opponent's low credibility witnesses whenever possible.

## § 5-6. Conclusions.

Communication strategy is an important aspect of any overall trial strategy. We have seen that by using a basic model of communication the process of sending persuasive messages to jurors can be broken down into five basic components: the sender, the receiver, the message, the channel, and feedback. The attorneys are the basic senders of persuasive messages in a trial, and communications strategy centers on what attorneys can do to be effective in this role. Jurors as message receivers are initially an unknown in the equation. One of the basic objectives in small group research is to develop knowledge about jurors and how they are going to exercise their function as message receivers.

One of the most valuable contributions of communication psychology to litigation has been to focus attention on the message as a distinct element in a communication. By studying specific messages like opening statements, witness testimony, and graphic exhibits, and the way they influence jurors, we can solve the two basic problems of all communication. These are making certain that the message sent and the message received are the same and that the persuasive intent of the message has been fulfilled.

# CHAPTER 6

# PSYCHOLOGICAL STRATEGIES IN VOIR DIRE



A consideration of psychological strategies in voir dire must begin with the recognition that the rules governing the conduct of voir dire vary from place to place and from court to court. Typically, judges in Federal court control voir dire and may or may not allow attorney participation. In some state courts, such as those in New York and Texas, voir dire is an open-ended process in which attorneys are permitted wide latitude in questioning prospective jurors. This does not, however, imply that in Federal courts the strategic implications of voir dire are completely negated. Many Federal judges will entertain the use of suggested voir dire questions.

There are two essential reasons for asking questions in voir dire. Questions can be asked because it is important to know the answers. Questions can also be asked because it is important to communicate something to the jurors through the questions. Voir dire, then, is actually the process of assessing the responses of prospective jurors as well as providing them with persuasive information.

## § 6-1. Juror Assessment.

Judgments made about jurors involve estimates as to how they are likely to behave with interest focused on the verdict they are likely to render. Secondarily, it will be important to evaluate the role jurors will play in the deliberation process. To many non-lawyers, the term "jury selection" implies selecting the jurors that you want. In actuality, of course, jury selection really means juror elimination. That is, exercising a limited number of challenges in order to remove jurors from the panel. Voir dire is largely a process of identifying jurors who, for a variety of reasons, will be wrong for the case. It is essentially an exercise of looking for "the wrong people." A particular juror may be an inappropriate candidate for a wide variety of reasons. The individual may possess intractable bias or prejudice against one of the litigants. Intensely held values, attitudes, and beliefs may exist which will have the tendency to interfere with a fair and impartial evaluation of testimony and other evidence. Finally, the trial lawyer may simply dislike the juror for idiosyncratic reasons of his own.

While trial lawyers are generally comfortable structuring their own voir dire questions and assessing the verbal component (*what* is said) of the prospective juror's answer, most are less experienced at analyzing paralinguistic cues (*how* it is said, such as pauses, stuttering, tone, pitch, and breathing patterns), and kinetic cues (body language, such as posture, gestures, facial expressions, and eye contact). Herein lies a wealth of information not attainable from the verbal component of communication. Whereas verbal behavior is used to communicate events external to the speaker, paralinguistic and nonverbal cues are used to express emotions and anxiety. Furthermore, true feelings are more easily assessed through nonverbal communication when deception is taking place. While we can often deceive with the words we choose, it is much more difficult to prevent our inner feelings from "leaking" through our nonverbal behavior. In recognition of this, some attorneys have begun to use trained observers to assess these subtle clues to a potential juror's biases and beliefs.

The principal objective of voir dire questions is to encourage jurors to reveal relevant information about themselves. Jurors tend to present certain images of themselves in voir dire which are self-flattering, or even self-aggrandising. This is particularly true when questions are psychologically or socially threatening. Responses to questions may also reflect a bias toward either wanting or not wanting to serve on the jury. Jurors who want to serve will try to avoid offending attorneys for either side. Where the rules governing voir dire are liberal, a number of different questioning techniques are available to help assess jurors.

## § 6-1(A). Questioning Techniques.

In cases where voir dire is expected to go on at length, projective questions can provide very useful insights into what jurors believe and how they are likely to react. Projective questions are those in which jurors are asked to talk in general terms about some person, experience, or event which serves as a stimulus. In reacting to this stimulus, jurors may provide subconscious or unguarded responses reflecting their attitudes, values and beliefs, patterns of motivation, and personality. These responses can then be evaluated against pretrial juror research findings.

When voir dire is more limited and it is necessary to use a small number of focused questions in the most efficient manner, areas of inquiry should be tied directly to behavioral variables found to be positively correlated with salient case issues. The development and testing of these questions can be undertaken with a variety of research techniques prior to trial.

When the opportunity to ask questions in voir dire is severely limited, or non-existent as it is in many Federal courts, the information that lawyers need to obtain about jurors is obviously restricted. In these situations, attorneys have to rely upon whatever knowledge they can obtain about the panel from whatever source. This is frequently limited to nonverbal behavior. Clinical psychologists have developed a number of techniques of passive observation. People trained in the area of participant observer, research and unobtrusive measures can detect many details of human behavior of a nonverbal character that normally escape the attention of other people. Such an observer stationed in the courtroom during voir dire can contribute helpful insights to the attorneys conducting the examination of jurors. It might be noted, for example, that several prospective jurors have indicated a strong desire for social acceptance through nonverbal actions like excessive smiling and head nodding. Other potential behaviors such as passivity, aggression, depression, feeling of inferiority, and alienation can be frequently detected. While observations of nonverbal behavior are important tools at the lawyer's disposal, they must be used with caution. The kinds of data available from courtroom observation provide global and generalized impressions of jurors at best. Whether or not observed characteristics are in any way related to a juror's evaluation of evidence, perception of testimony, or to the ultimate verdict is unknown without having undertaken prior research.

## § 6-1(B). Looking for Inconsistencies in Juror Behavior.

Jurors, like other people on public display, will endeavor to present a positive or attractive image of themselves. It is useful to analyze and interpret this image in terms of inconsistencies and contradictions which signal things the juror wishes not to reveal. These inconsistencies can include words and how they are used, or discerned by reading between the lines of what a juror does or says. Inconsistencies can also be detected in a juror's attire or physical appearance. People who wish to avoid being labeled as blue collar workers may "dress up" for court. Careful observation of style and coordination of the individual's clothing may suggest that in his everyday life, this person is not the person he appears to be in the courtroom. In a recent trial, a juror described himself as a food handling technician, thereby making himself acceptable to attorneys who felt that people with technical backgrounds would be favorable to their side. A post-trial interview revealed that the juror was, in fact, a busboy in a hotel. In this instance, as in many others, there is a natural tendency among jurors to inflate their position in life. They are not telling lies, but they can indeed deceive. One of the ways to avoid being beguiled by what jurors say is to carefully observe inconsistencies between what they say and the signs or signals of behavior.

## § 6-2. Identifying Punitive Jurors.

Attempts to identify the characteristics of punitive jurors have been frustrating at best. Traditionally, lawyers have tended to focus on surface traits or observable characteristics of jurors which were thought to be stereotypically associated with punitive jurors. The characteristics most frequently employed are demographically based; that is, characteristics of jurors associated with their age, race, sex, level of education, and occupation. In an effort to assess the reliability of demographic predictors of punitive dispositions, Litigation Sciences, has undertaken numerous studies to determine the extent to which these punitive jurors can be differentiated or identified in some specific way. In all of these research efforts, emphasis has been placed on developing models to assist trial lawyers more accurately predict punitive jurors during the voir dire and to develop effective case presentation to ameliorate the otherwise explosive potential of a jury containing punitive jurors who could not be eliminated for cause or struck with peremptory challenges.

To date, Litigation Sciences has conducted interviews with more than 14,000 people either in post-trial interviews in jurisdictions where we are permitted to talk with jurors or in pretrial research activities undertaken for specific clients. The statistical analysis of this massive database has revealed that demographic characteristics are exceedingly poor predictors of verdict predisposition in general and for the propensity to award punitive damages in particular. This finding is really not surprising. Psychologists have known for years that the decisions that people make in any decision-making environment are a function of the values, attitudes, and beliefs that are contained in the decision maker's cognitive structure. In a juror context, what people believe to be and the personal experiences that they have had are obviously more important in helping them form opinions and conclusions about the character of litigants, matters of fact, or issues of evaluation than are, for example, their weight, their age, or their sex. As a case in point, of all of the demographic data collected in our studies, only one demographic variable has been found to be statistically associated with jury verdict. Correlation analysis reveals that women are slightly more likely than men to award punitive damages. No other demographic variable has any statistical or even practical relevance to identifying punitive jurors.

If demographic variables are unreliable predictors of punitive jurors, are there any other measures or characteristics of these people that can be employed to assist the trial attorney in jury selection? Clearly, we know that these people exist; can they be identified by observable characteristics? Fortunately, the answer to this question is yes! In fact, we have discovered that there are several highly reliable indicia of punitive damage predispositions, and these have been successfully employed in simulated research environments as well as used in actual court cases. These characteristics are behavioral in nature and relate to the psychological and sociological characteristics of people who sit on juries.

## § 6-2(A). The Psychology of Punitive Jurors.

One psychological variable which we found to have strong associations with punitive damages is the emotional state of depression. Clinical psychologists typically deal with depressive personalities as a mental health problem. However, we have witnessed repeated incidences of punitive jurors frequently manifesting indications of depression. To accurately diagnose depression from a medical or clinical perspective requires very specialized training and experience. Nevertheless, there are a number of signs or traits that trial lawyers can use. These include facial expressions, posture, eye contact, and responsiveness to questions from either the attorney or the judge.

In extreme cases, all of us are capable of observing people who could be defined as psychologically or emotionally depressed. In those extreme cases where a depressed individual is easily observed and recognized, there is a high probability of that person awarding punitive damages should the jury find against the defendant. What about instances where depression is latent and not observable without the assistance of trained specialists? Fortunately, behavioral scientists have learned that there are specific instances in the lives of most people which normally result in depression or anxiety. Some of these are psychological in nature, and others are more sociological in nature.

*Death and Dying.* Most human beings faced with the death or imminent loss of a loved one or close friend experience depression. In fact, most psychologists agree that otherwise normal and psychologically healthy people require about two years to recover from the death of a loved one. Hence, where appropriate, voir dire questions should be addressed to this area of the juror's personal life whenever possible. This is particularly critical in personal injury or death cases. If a juror indicates that he or she has personally suffered any sort of personal or family tragedy, or social trauma, the juror should be scrutinized with great care and caution.

*Divorce/Separation.* Jurors who reveal that they have recently been divorced or are in the process of obtaining a divorce or separation, represent a punitive threat. Interestingly enough, this is particularly important in the case of middle-aged men. Dissolution of a long-term marriage and family structure is very difficult for most people. This situation can be particularly devastating when the male partner has not initiated the termination of the marriage relationship. When placed in a position to make judgments or evaluations, these jurors frequently possess feelings of resentment or bitterness and are willing to lash out at other people when provided an opportunity to do so.

Trial lawyers are well-advised to exercise great caution with middle-aged people who are recently divorced or separated if punitive damages are a significant threat in the litigation.

*Professional or Occupational Trauma.* People who have suffered severe ego-assaultive experiences relating to their job, occupation, or profession are potentially dangerous jurors. Not unlike jurors described in the divorce scenario above, these people are typically angry, frustrated, and oftentimes experience deep feelings of inner humiliation and embarrassment. If the trial attorney discovers during voir dire that a particular juror is unemployed, it is very important to explore this issue. Obviously, this must be done with sensitivity to avoid exacerbating the underlying cause of potential antagonism and hostility.

Very frequently, the spouse of an individual who has lost his or her job may experience even greater feelings of anxiety and depression than the individual who has actually been fired or displaced. The wife of a middle-age executive who has lost his job may possess feelings of guilt over her frustration, resentment, or bitterness associated with her husband and his predicament. Once again, post-trial interviews frequently reveal that these people are strong proponents for the awarding of punitive damages.

## § 6-2(B). Sociological Variables.

In addition to these psychological characteristics frequently associated with punitive damages, there are four significant sociological predictors of people predisposed to award punitive damages. These conditions are referred to as anomie, locus of control, and occupational underemployment.

*Anomie.* Sociologists define anomie as a condition existing in a society where people experience a sense of normlessness. That is, people are confused as to "the rules of the game" and their roles as individuals in society.

When people lose a sense of understanding as to where they fit in or how their personal role relates to the overall social structure, they often experience feelings of frustration and anxiety. When people, for example, feel that "life has passed them by," "that they've been left behind or left out," "that they played by the rules but haven't been rewarded," they frequently experience a generalized and non-specific hostility referred to as anomie. In a post-trial interview with a 60-year-old male juror who was singularly responsible for the imposition of a huge punitive award against a major pharmaceutical company, we discovered precisely this phenomenon. This life-long blue collar worker expressed criticism, antagonism, and hostility toward the defendant, and yet he could not accurately be described as "anti-corporation." In fact, he displayed intense antagonism and frustration not only with large corporations, but also with the government, politicians, labor unions, teenagers, Blacks, and Jews. This particular juror felt that he had worked hard all of his life, had followed the rules, and had failed to receive any of the attendant rewards allegedly associated with the prescribed social norms of society. This man's generalized frustrations with significant social institutions were clearly focused on the defendant in the lawsuit. Serving on the jury permitted him an opportunity to vent his frustrations and antagonisms on a clearly defined social entity.

Can a lawyer detect the existence of anomie during voir dire? There are indeed a number of question areas which will sensitize lawyers to the existence of anomie. These include questions relating to life satisfaction in general, that is, questions designed to ascertain the individual's general description of his feelings of satisfaction and happiness with his personal, social, and family life.

*Locus of Control.* A second important sociological variable found to be associated with punitive damage verdicts is a concept referred to as locus of control. Locus of control defines the extent to which people perceive the nature and extent of control that they possess in their own lives. Some people feel that they can conquer any objective and possess a confidence in their own ability to master adversity and pursue opportunities. These people are referred to as having a high internal locus of control. On the other hand, there are people who feel that external events shape their lives and their significant events. These people frequently explain that "luck or fate" was responsible for serious negative or positive events in their lives and that "things just happen to the individual." These people are described as having a high external locus of control.

When a juror perceives that his or her life has been characterized by external events (frequently bad luck), he or she becomes a good candidate for awarding punitive damages. Voir dire questions relating to locus of control can be formulated in terms of: (1) job stability; (2) the relationship between the juror's education and current occupation or employment; (3) the juror's level of contentment or satisfaction with his or her current life situation; and (4) general expectations about the future.

*Occupational Underemployment.* Occupational underemployment can exist at two levels. The first is represented by a juror's current occupation or job being inconsistent with that individual's level of education or training. As an example, an individual with a master's degree in art history who is working as a clerk in a grocery store or as a cab driver would be defined as underemployed. Another example might be a juror who majored in elementary education in college and is unable to secure employment as a teacher. Research has demonstrated that when placed in a jury environment, these people frequently become punitive jurors.

The second classification of occupational underemployment can be described as job or occupational inconsistency within the mind of the individual. That is, these people *believe in their own minds* that they ought to have a better job, a higher position, or more authority. The reality of many cases is that these people are already at a level of maximum capability or performance.

Perceptually underemployed jurors are the Archie Bunkers of the world. They frequently dominate their family and close personal and social relationships but fail to receive the external social reward and reinforcement to which they feel they are entitled. In many instances, these people proceed through life with feelings of generalized frustration and antagonism that can be leveled at a defendant in a law suit. This is particularly the case when the defendant represents a large company or some other entity with which the juror can associate his perceived lack of social reward, external gratification, and recognition.

## § 6-3. Techniques of Persuasion in Voir Dire.

Voir dire functions traditionally and primarily as a means of selecting and rejecting jurors. However, it also represents the only opportunity for jurors to directly interact with counsel or the judge who communicates counsel's queries. As such, it provides a unique opportunity for the presentation of one's case. The experienced attorney recognizes that the trial does not begin in earnest with the opening statement. Indeed, juror perceptions are amenable to influence from the moment the jurors enter the courtroom.

Various techniques of persuasion can be employed in voir dire. These include juror self-persuasion, forced compliance, sensitization, inoculation, and techniques which warn of the opponent's persuasive intent.

## § 6-3(A). Inducing Juror Self-Persuasion.

Social psychologists know that there are various circumstances under which people become self-persuaders. Among jurors, self-persuasion can take place when jurors make up their minds, or reach conclusions, without being directly persuaded to do so by an external message or communication specifically directed at leading them to this conclusion. What seems to occur in cases of self-persuasion is that jurors suddenly become aware of something "they knew all along." Jurors may emerge from a state of doubt into a state of certainty regarding some issue. They will spontaneously realize that they have reached a conclusion about something they had previously not considered.

One of the most striking kinds of self-persuasion occurs when a set of attitudes or beliefs appears to be firmly in place and information counter to these attitudes is suddenly presented in an unexpected way. Initially, there will be strong resistance to this information, but somehow a nagging doubt will have been planted, and after a time lag the attitudes which resist the information suddenly crumble and disappear. This is particularly likely to occur in the wake of the kind of strong frontal attack which can be presented in the form of a voir dire question or set of questions. There will be strong initial resistance, but inroads will have been made. A given juror may continue to be disturbed by the attack but ultimately integrate the new information into his cognitive structure.

Frontal attacks using counter-attitudinal information, or information which contradicts existing attitudes and beliefs, are particularly appropriate to voir dire. They have the best chance of success when they are based on some incontrovertible fact which cannot be ignored. Attitude change comes after a delay and occurs because new information has forced a rearranging of cognitive structures within a juror's mind. The key to why this works and the reason why it is appropriate to voir dire is that jurors must not be aware that an attempt is being made to persuade them. The attitude change occurs because jurors are unaware of the working of any outside influence or stimulus. They are convinced that they have changed their minds by themselves.

Since self-persuasion is a delayed process which takes place within a juror's mind, it can often be set in motion by a rapid "hit and run" attack, a rhetorical thrust, or the almost surreptitious planting of a key piece of information. Knowledge of self-persuasion techniques, combined with the knowledge that the proper attitude context may exist, makes voir dire a good opportunity for using self-persuasion strategies.

### § 6-3(B). Forced Compliance Through Induced Role Playing.

Social psychologists have established that people often come to know their own attitudes, beliefs, and feelings about something through the observation of their own behavior. Thus, through their own self-perceptions, jurors can sometimes be led to express an attitude or belief they did not know they had. Having heard themselves express the thought, they will later be willing to defend it. The theory of attitude change or reinforcement through self-persuasion can often be used in voir dire. Jurors can be led to make admissions which are consistent with the position of one of the litigants. When they do so, they will have psychologically positioned themselves to cognitively defend an attitude that might have been previously neutral, flexible, or ambiguous.

The most effective way to modify attitudes through self-persuasion theory is to induce jurors to play a role. When people play a role, they are often doing something with which they are initially uncomfortable. They may, for example, be forcing themselves to say something they do not really believe. It is often possible in voir dire to induce jurors to play roles and, in doing so, force them to comply with a position they would otherwise avoid. Roles which are at variance with what people think they believe are called attitude discrepant. When jurors assume a role which is attitude discrepant, they may change the underlying attitude so that what they believe is now in conformity with what they are doing. Their attitude changes because of the well-known fact that people are more likely to believe something when they hear themselves saying it than when they hear someone else saying it.

There are many commonplace examples of the "try it, you'll like it" syndrome. Self-persuasion techniques involving role playing are often used, for example, with children who shy away from the unfamiliar, whether it be a food or some new experience. "Think how much you're going to like this," the mother will say as she tries to persuade her child to do something he doesn't want to do.

Two points can be made about the matter of attitude change through role playing. First, people are often persuaded to change attitudes toward something by observing their own behavior when playing a role. Second, people are more likely to learn, or change attitudes, when they adopt the role voluntarily than when they feel they are being pressured to do so. Studies have shown that even thinking about playing a role can bring about a modification in attitude. If a juror can be made to see himself doing something, for example, it will increase the possibility of his doing it. When someone goes from making the statement, "I could never do that," to the statement, "I could see myself doing that," there has already been an attitude change.

Voir dire offers numerous opportunities to induce juror role playing in a way that will force compliance with a particular attitude or belief. A defense attorney might ask the following question in voir dire:

> Put yourself in the place of people who work for Company X who have tried their best to manufacture products with the highest standards of quality and then find yourself accused of making something defective and harmful to people. Do you think that because someone is injured using a product, there must be something wrong with the product?

In a contract dispute, a plaintiff attorney might ask:

> Put yourself in the place of Mr. Johnson. He thought he had a deal; he shook hands on it. Is there anyone in this courtroom who doesn't believe that major corporations have the duty to behave according to the standard of honesty and integrity that people like you and I do?

## § 6-3(C). Group Sensitization.

It is often possible to use self-persuasion techniques on the part of the entire jury panel to modify an attitude or belief, or to plant a new idea. Sometimes, through a series of questions, the panel can be sensitized to an argument. This occurred in a recent case involving a sudden and unexpected automobile accident in which a driver lost control of his car. Plaintiff alleged that the blowout of a tire had occurred because it had been defectively manufactured. Counsel for the defense wished to make the point that there are numerous alternative explanations for what happened. Defense counsel also wanted the jurors to make an internal causal attribution, that is, to blame the driver for what happened. To induce this kind of attribution, the attorneys suggested that what happened in this case is not what would happen to most people in this situation. Jurors were immediately sensitized to this line of defense in voir dire through a series of questions. The attorney asked:

> How many of you drive? (All raised their hands.)
> How many of you ever had a flat tire? (All raised their hands.)
> How many of you have had a blowout? (All raised their hands.)
> How many of you have lost control of your car in this situation? (None raised their hands.)

With this simple series of questions, the case for the defense was presented in microcosm.

### § 6-3(D). Warning Jurors of the Opponent's Persuasive Intent.

There are many instances in our lives in which we observe someone trying to change someone else's opinion with a persuasive message. When this is particularly overt, people normally become very sensitive to these efforts. Evidence shows that we are less likely to be persuaded by a speech, taped message, or written appeal if we think it is designed to influence our opinions than when we do not possess such knowledge.

Jurors resist persuasive messages when they have prior knowledge of the intent to persuade. This is particularly true for attitudes they consider important. Prior warning sets in motion the formulation of counter-arguments. These counter-arguments are then in place when the persuasive message arrives.

Voir dire is an appropriate time to warn jurors that they are going to be subject to various arguments from the other side during the course of the trial. We may know, for example, that certain juror attitudes are likely to be aligned in opposition to the case for the other side. Often, the results of pretrial research into juror attitudes can be usefully employed in this connection.

Suppose, for example, the case involves a contract dispute. Our client, the defendant, has been accused of failing to perform alleged contractual obligations. It will be argued that these obligations were not the intent of the contract. A voir dire question might ask:

> The plaintiff is going to claim that this contract obligated my client to provide for the maintenance of the flood control system after the installations were in place. Do you feel that you'll be able to evaluate this contract objectively and find out what it really says?

With this, and related kinds of questions, jurors will have been forewarned about the plaintiff's principal arguments. They will have an opportunity to begin formulating counter-arguments in their minds at the same time they state they can "be objective."

### § 6-3(E). Inoculation.

Inoculation against the opponent's opening arguments is another effective, though underused, voir dire strategy. In this regard, research on attitude change has shown that persuasive attacks on unquestioned beliefs (those beliefs for which the juror has no alternative viewpoint) can be astonishingly effective when the belief has gone unchallenged for some time. Self-generated counter-arguments (arguments raised by the listener to counter the position of the speaker) will be weak during this kind of attack, and the listener will be highly susceptible to persuasion. This is of particular concern when trial strategy depends heavily upon attitudes jurors are expected to bring with them into the courtroom. The possibility exists that a direct assault upon favorable attitudes by the opposition will succeed in creating confusion, doubt, and the eventual abandonment of the jurors' original position. This threat can be reduced by inoculating arguments which may come later in the trial.

Inoculation is most effective when a mild attack on a belief is supplemented with counter-arguments that a juror may not easily generate on his own. For example, suppose a company is being sued for allegedly manufacturing a defective airplane involved in a fatal accident. One argument for the defense could be that, "The FAA has approved and certified this airplane for production and use." Although most people have a generally high regard for the FAA, they know little about it and have had little need to defend their opinions about it. This kind of unquestioned belief is highly vulnerable to effective counter-arguments that derogate the competence of the FAA. The defense could inoculate against these attacks by asking:

> Some people think that all federal agencies are inefficient and bureaucratic; but is there anyone here who does not believe that the FAA rigorously reviewed this airplane before it was put on the market? Is there anyone here who does not believe the FAA is concerned about and dedicated to the lives of the traveling public?

Several queries along these lines would provide the necessary inoculation against attacks on unquestioned beliefs. Thus, a mild dose of the plaintiff's "virus," supplemented by the defense's "antibiotics," will help develop stronger defenses that can deal with a more potent attack at a later time.

Another example of inoculation can be seen in a feminine hygiene products case in which the defendant-manufacturer was a very old, reliable, and highly regarded company. Pretrial research had established that the jury panel as a whole would be positively disposed toward the defendant. Many jurors remembered the company's products from their own childhood. The research further revealed that jurors would possess the belief that the company had upheld a particular kind of trust which is fundamental to its responsibility as a producer of household baby products. The defense counsel felt that plaintiff would wage a strong attack on this attitude-belief constellation in the opening statement.

Since the defense suspected that positive attitudes among jurors would be based more on a "halo" effect of positive childhood memories than on any factual substance and that these beliefs had gone unexamined for many years, there was concern that plaintiff's attack might succeed. In order to guard against this possibility, the defense elected to launch a mild attack on the beliefs in question, supplemented with counter-arguments that jurors would not be able to readily generate on their own.

The defendant had carefully constructed an image in the public mind of compassion and reliability, mainly through the sale of its baby products. There was a long standing, ongoing advertising campaign based on these values. Plaintiff was going to allege that the company had been deliberately negligent in marketing a line of products without knowing whether or not they would be dangerous to the user. The defense knew that the plaintiff would put forward the argument that the company had acted precipitously, without adequate testing, in order to maintain its market share. By implication, the company management was governed by pure profit motive and a disregard for the welfare of its customers. In this case, the defense used voir dire questions like the following:

> There's a lot of cynicism about big business today, and there are no doubt a fair number of people who think there's a wide gap between the advertising image of a company and its actual business practices. Do you think you can lay aside some of these current ideas and judge this case on its merits?
>
> The plaintiff is going to ask you to believe that a company like Bates and Hubbard which has enjoyed the public trust for over fifty years would suddenly throw out its standards of quality. Are you willing to look at the record without prejudice in this matter and see that the record speaks for itself?
>
> It's hard to believe that anyone would think that a company which has been dedicated for generations to making products like Bates and Hubbard baby powder, Bates and Hubbard baby oil, and numerous other products would suddenly take leave of its senses and enter the market with an untested, dangerous product. Are you willing to consider the possibility that what happened to the plaintiff had no connection with Bates and Hubbard products at all? Are you willing to look at this matter with no prejudice toward the defendant?

For effective inoculation, a number of queries along these lines should provide the necessary protection against attacks on the jurors' unquestioned positive attitude-belief regarding the defendant and its products.

In sum, inoculation, like the other persuasive techniques discussed here, is part of an effort in voir dire to get jurors to psychologically position themselves to cognitively defend attitudes favorable to our side.

## § 6-3(F). Self-Perception Theory.

Self-perception theory offers another voir dire strategy for altering more neutral and ambiguous beliefs. The application of this theory is straightforward. For example, the defense could question a particular juror along the following lines: "Mrs. Smith, do you believe that consumer advocates are sometimes overzealous or just plain wrong in their attacks on some products?" Jurors responding positively to this kind of question will leave the voir dire with new skepticism about consumer advocates. Thus, by observing their own responses to the attorney's carefully worded questions, they will conclude that they do not strongly believe everything said by consumer advocates.

## § 6-4. Voir Dire: The Elimination Decision.

It was stated earlier that voir dire is an exercise in finding the "wrong" jurors. This means evaluating what each juror as an individual brings with him into the courtroom. It also means assessing how each person will fit into the group in which he will be placed.

At times, a juror must be eliminated strictly on the basis of individual characteristics, but more often than not, the decision will also incorporate an assessment of how much these characteristics are likely to matter in the context of a group. This is because individual traits are subject to group influence, and through this influence individual traits can be muted or exaggerated. Just how this will occur will depend upon the personality and motivational characteristics of all the jurors and how they interact.

Suppose a juror has cognitive structures in place which are unfavorable to our side. Whether this juror should be eliminated depends upon how much these cognitive structures will matter in the context of the group. Suppose the individual is a passive, follower type, with low self-esteem. Such a person will probably be led to a verdict by other jurors. Hence, it may not be necessary to eliminate this juror.

The capacity of a juror to form extended psychological relationships with other jurors, attorneys, and the litigants may also take precedence over the operation of cognitive structure. A feeling of affiliation or liking may lead a juror to subordinate certain cognitions and make decisions on the basis of these affiliations. On the other hand, a juror with a weak favorable cognitive structure may have to be eliminated because it is clear that this individual will have strong feelings of aversion toward the attorney for our side, or toward the litigant. Racial or class prejudice is an example of this kind of aversion.

In choosing jurors by a process of elimination, it is necessary to decide how much a particular juror can hurt. This will be a decision based on individual juror characteristics and the role a juror is likely to play in the dynamic of the juror group decision-making process.

## § 6-5. Conclusions.

The basic purpose of voir dire is juror selection, but voir dire must also be viewed as an initial opportunity to present the case in microcosm and to begin the process of persuading jurors. Psychological techniques of persuasion, like those proposed here, can be employed in a variety of ways. Once the general thrust of the case has been determined, and pretrial research is complete, it is possible to map out voir dire strategy that will effectively achieve the dual purpose of choosing a favorable jury and presenting the main outlines of the case to follow.

Psychological research offers a number of helpful suggestions that taken together improve typical voir dire strategies. More efficient use of paralinguistic and kinetic cues will aid in detecting true juror feelings. Further, carefully selected questions in voir dire can inoculate jurors who may be susceptible to attacks on previously unchallenged beliefs. Finally, jurors led to make an admission that is consistent with the position of one of the litigants will "psychologically position" themselves to cognitively defend an attitude that was previously neutral, flexible, or ambiguous.

# CHAPTER 7

# JUROR SELECTION STRATEGY



Jury selection is one of the most challenging and complex applications of the social sciences to litigation. Depending upon the particular jurisdiction, background information on prospective jurors may be quite limited, and lawyers may also be required to exercise their selection decisions in a short period of time. Where lawyers have wider discretion with voir dire, there are still, nevertheless, severe limitations on the ability to learn very much about the people seated in the jury box. The judge and/or lawyer can ask questions, but jurors clearly control what *they* want the questioner to know.

## § 7-1. Juror Selection: The Primary Approach.

Lawyer experience with jurors in the venue is the basic starting point of any juror selection strategy. Most trial attorneys possess "feelings," "hunches," "gut feelings," or "instincts" about the type of people they want or wish to avoid for a particular case. For the most part, these views are based on stereotypes about human behavior. While these may be unscientific and impressionistic, they represent an inventory of beliefs about people based on past observation. These ideas are important because the trial lawyer must be comfortable and self-confident with his audience. But these feelings may or may not accurately reflect the ultimate behavior of a given juror in a particular case. When properly employed, behavioral science research and courtroom observation techniques can assist the lawyer to confirm or reject instincts and perceptions about prospective jurors.

If, for example, an attorney feels that middle-aged housewives will be positively predisposed to his client, this can be tested in a research setting. If he feels that blue collar workers will be antagonistic toward him or his clients, this can be tested as well. Thus, the primary approach to juror selection is one in which behavioral science research and lawyer intuitions are juxtaposed. However, juror selection strategy should not be limited solely to testing lawyer impressions about jurors. These impressions are a starting point. Many other hypotheses based on concepts and theories about human behavior with which lawyers may be unfamiliar can be subjected to empirical verification. Pretrial research aimed at developing juror selection strategies will generally pursue a complex program of investigation into both the psychological and sociological characteristics of jurors and how these will influence the outcome of the trial. A description of these juror research techniques will be presented later in Chapter 9.

Juror selection decisions really represent the lawyer's predictions as to how members of the panel will arrive at their ultimate verdict. This, of course, implies an evaluation of individual people as well as an assessment about how these people will operate as a part of a decision-making group. Hence, jury selection must include considerations of potential jurors at two levels: the psychological and the sociological. Psychological characteristics are the traits jurors display as individuals. Sociological characteristics consist of the traits jurors display as members of a group. Verdicts represent a unique form of human decision making. Clearly, the decision of a group is not the mere amalgamation of individual decisions. Thus, juror selection strategies must also involve a consideration of social class memberships, cultural and sub-cultural identifications, and concepts about how individuals function in a decision-making environment. It will be useful to look at these factors in greater detail.

## § 7-2. Psychological Characteristics.

In addition to the cognitions that jurors bring with them into the courtroom, it is important to think about prospective jurors in terms of a number of psychological variables like motivation, personality characteristics, and the feelings jurors have about themselves. Each of these concepts has been investigated in great detail in university research settings. Much of what has been learned can be helpful in assessing how jurors will do the things they do in the courtroom and during deliberations.

### § 7-2(A). Motivation.

Human behavior is not random or accidental. It proceeds with certain motivations and goals in mind. Motivation propels action and stimulates the individual to engage in some behavior. Jurors, as human beings, possess general motivational patterns. Their behavior will be consistent with these patterns. Motivation involves self-protection, the gratification of needs, the reduction of tension, and the enhancement of the individual and his concept of self. Jurors are actuated by all of these motives when they come into court.

An important element in jury selection is the discovery of the extent to which juror behavior is linked to certain general patterns of motivation. Although there is not complete agreement among psychologists as to the nature of motivation, most accept the idea that certain needs are fundamental and that they probably exist in some sort of hierarchy. Motivation grows out of this hierarchy of needs in individuals and even in entire societies. Basic physiological needs, like the need for food, water, and safety, must be gratified before other "higher" needs emerge. These higher needs will include the need for love and affection and a need to feel a part of some group or society. When these needs have been fulfilled, still higher needs make their presence felt. Needs for self-respect, prestige, recognition, and achievement emerge. Finally, there is the need for self-actualization, or the belief on the part of a person that his or her potential is being fulfilled.

Jurors may be motivated to serve on a jury to achieve social recognition or prestige. Jury service may also provide the opportunity to fulfill needs associated with a social or political cause or some other set of intensely held beliefs. Once empaneled, jurors may, for example, pay attention to a particular witness or area of testimony because of motivational needs associated with learning new concepts or information.

Differences in motivational patterns among jurors can frequently be seen in the courtroom. Needs and the ways in which they are manifested among ghetto Blacks are very different from the way they are disposed among upper class Whites. These people will have entirely different approaches to life and may differ in the extreme when judging the motivations of litigation and of issues relating to equity and justice. At the same time, professional, college educated jurors will be motivated by different needs than blue collar, working class jurors. These differences will emerge in their expectations of the courtroom participants as well as in their expectations of other jurors. When various theories of motivation are considered, a number of important notions about jurors can be inferred and later incorporated into the jury selection process.

### § 7-2(B). Freud's Psychoanalytic Theory of Motivation.

One of the most important theories of human motivation is the psychoanalytic theory of Sigmund Freud. Freud's thinking has had a major impact on modern thought in general and is of particular importance for determining why people behave as they do. Freud emphasized the role of basic biological drives in motivation and argued that the way in which the personality becomes organized is a direct result of the need to gratify these basic drives or instincts. According to Freud, the personality which governs motivation is organized into three basic systems or processes. These are the *id,* the *superego,* and the *ego.* The id is comprised of biological drives generally defined as aggressive, destructive, pleasure-seeking impulses. The superego is made up of a system of moralistic inhibitions imposed on the id by parents and society. The ego is a mediating system which arbitrates the impulsive urges of the id and the suppressive nature of the superego. The conflicts which ensue among these three processes can lead to frustration and anxiety. The ego, or reality principle, seeks to cope with this frustration and anxiety through the use of a variety of mechanisms. These defense mechanisms as they are called often deny or distort reality in order to help the individual control or overrule internal motivations which are socially unacceptable. Defense mechanisms can also be used to resolve internal conflicts between the superego and the id. These conflict resolutions occur beneath a level of conscious recognition by the individual. One of the most important insights propounded by Freud is that a great deal of human behavior is determined by subconscious motivations.

The usefulness of Freudian insights for the study of juror behavior relates to understanding the existence of subconscious motivation and the use of defense mechanisms. A complete discussion of Freudian theory is beyond the scope of this book, but some of the defense mechanisms relevant to jury selection applications are identification, projection, displacement, and rationalization.

Identification is a very common and very powerful mechanism people use to copy and imitate others. If the individual is placed in a situation where his ego structure is rendered inadequate, the person may compensate by imitating someone else. For example, a juror with a low level of education and limited social or interpersonal experience may attempt to emulate jurors he considers to be more knowledgeable and sophisticated. The imitation of "opinion leaders" is common among jurors. It is important to identify the possible existence of jurors who could provide an opinion leadership role model and those who could become their followers.

In addition to the identification phenomenon occurring among members of the jury panel, attorneys should consider the possibility of extended influence. That is, identification occurring between a particular juror and a member of the trial team or a witness. This factor has been a significant influence in a number of cases in which Litigation Sciences has been involved in jury selection decisions.

A second defense mechanism is the phenomenon of projection. Projection is the opposite of identification. Projection consists of attributing to others motives and forms of behavior which the individual subconsciously recognizes as undesirable or unwanted within himself. This can be very dangerous when a juror views a litigant in this manner. Projection can often be the motivation behind certain kinds of causal attributions.

Displacement is a defense mechanism which transfers energy from one object to another. People who are underemployed in terms of their education and intelligence may be inclined to channel their frustration by blaming others for their plight. They may even blame a particular class of individuals. Some psychologists argue that one of the elements of racism is a displacement phenomenon: people find themselves dissatisfied with their own lives and find solace in blaming some racial group for their misfortunes. Displacement can also work in more subtle ways. A fight with one's spouse might be followed by a spending spree or some other form of impulsive behavior. Instead of directing energy against the other person, the energy is rechanneled into another form of unrelated behavior. Jurors may use displacement mechanisms as part of their motivation in rendering punitive verdicts. As an example, a juror who has lost a job or whose spouse has been fired may direct his anger and hostility toward a corporate defendant in a completely unrelated matter.

Finally, one of the most widespread of all defense mechanisms is the one called rationalization. Rationalization consists of providing ourselves with acceptable reasons for actions which are troubling, unacceptable, or in some way inexplicable. Pretrial research frequently reveals that jurors will have to engage in rationalizing behavior in order to render verdicts in certain cases. In traumatic personal injury cases, jurors may have to develop rationalization for awarding or refusing to award large damages to the plaintiff in order to protect the jurors' own sense of self-worth. Knowing in advance which kinds of people are likely to engage in which kinds of rationalization can be a critical element of jury selection strategy.

## § 7-2(C). Neo-Psychoanalytic Approaches.

Various disciples and critics of Freud have promulgated ideas about motivation which remain within the basic psychoanalytic framework of unconscious drives and the development of mechanisms for their gratification. Adler felt that all human motivation grows out of a fundamental need to establish superiority and to overcome childhood feelings of inferiority. Fromm argued that all of our behavior is motivated by a need to overcome a certain existential loneliness, while Sullivan put forth the idea that all of our motivation should be understood in terms of the drive to form relationships with others.

Although none of these theories of motivation offers a complete explanation for all juror behavior, they are often suggestive of how certain jurors will behave in certain situations. Loneliness is a good example. While everyone suffers the pangs of loneliness and estrangement on occasion, the problem is particularly acute for people who have suffered the death of a loved one, for single people living in strange cities, or for divorced jurors forced to live alone for the first time.

In one of the IBM antitrust cases, an elderly, divorced juror felt intense anxiety and depression over the ending of the trial. This individual had come to view a number of the pro-IBM jurors as "close friends" who provided "affection and support." Interestingly enough, post-trial interviews revealed that those other jurors viewed the lonely divorcee as a social isolate who had little interaction with the rest of the jury and was "never really a member of the group but would vote the right way."

Jurors who exhibit certain traits, like loneliness, often play a key role in the jury both because of their motivation to deal with other jurors in particular ways and through the processes by which they are motivated to perceive issues in the trial.

## § 7-2(D). Other Motivations Found Among Jurors.

Jurors are likely to possess many different motives which, individually or in various combinations, may be aroused during the course of the trial. When pretrial research indicates that certain motives are associated with significant aspects of the case, a careful scrutiny of potential jurors along these dimensions becomes a critical element of selection strategy. Some of the more frequently encountered motives observed in our work for clients over the years include the desire for social approval and status, the need for security, the pursuit of personal interest or curiosity, the drive for self-realization, and the need to give and receive affection.

*Social Approval.* Jurors are often motivated by the need for social approval and status. For example, jurors who possess a great need for social approval will frequently dress and behave in ways conforming to their perceptions of social standards. This may include displays of excessive formality or politeness, or exacting attention to personal grooming and attire. In a series of product liability cases, psychologists at Litigation Sciences were concerned about precisely this characteristic. One important element comprising the overall profile of desirable juror types for our client included certain characteristics of middle-aged women. In addition to other criteria, we were very interested in identifying women jurors in this age bracket who displayed fastidious attention to the coordination of their clothing, makeup, and adorning jewelry. While attire itself was *not* a predictor variable, it was a good surrogate reflecting a basic need (social approval) that was indeed correlated with verdict predisposition.

Status is related to social approval, but status is a form of social approval in which one's superiority over others is acknowledged. This may involve being able to wield power over others, command wealth and possessions, or receive deference from others. Identifying jurors who are motivated by high status needs may be important because of an association with courtroom perceptions and/or verdict predisposition. At the same time, such needs can be a good predictor of potential relationships among members of the jury panel.

*The Need for Security.* The need for security is commonly found as a basis for motivation in juror behavior. People with a prominent need for security feel that they must protect themselves and their loved ones both physically and/or psychologically. If testing issues or compliance with standards are expected to play a predominant role in the trial, it may be critical to identify jurors who possess this characteristic. This can also be true in matters involving allegations of financial, medical, or legal negligence or malpractice.

*Curiosity.* The pursuit of personal interests and curiosity seeking are motivations displayed by jurors at one time or another. Quite often a juror will have a personal interest in some salient aspect of the trial. An engineer might have an interest in design procedures and find this interest stimulated in a patent case. The engineer might be motivated to assert his interest and thereby become an "expert witness" during deliberation and possibly dominate other jurors. In a childbirth defect case, a nurse might have a personal interest in some arcane aspect of genetics. And, even though she may lack an accurate understanding of the topic, her professed mastery of the testimony presented in the trial combined with her formal credentials may allow her to exert a distorted influence on other jurors. People with intense personal interests in a trial often turn out to be particularly dangerous to one side or another.

*Self-Realization.* A few jurors may wish to serve on a jury as an exercise in self-realization. They want to achieve some personal goal by serving on the jury. They may be anxious to convict or anxious to award damages. They may wish to achieve intellectual satisfactions of some kind through service as a juror. Through use of certain questions, juror research can identify potential jurors highly motivated by the need to achieve self-realization and predict how this kind of motivation may be linked to verdict predisposition in a particular trial.

*Need for Affection.* Jurors who are motivated by a strong need to give and receive affection may also play a special role in a given case. These people may react to courtroom events through the feelings they have for one of the attorneys or one of the litigants. They can also play a unique role in the group dynamics of the deliberations by spending their time seeking approval and affection from the other jurors.

While motives may be difficult to assess by untrained observers, they are an important element in the overall evaluation of potential jurors.

## § 7-2(E). Personality.

A second major psychological construct that must be included in any evaluation of potential jurors is the concept of personality. While there is a wide variety of conflicting and oftentimes competing theories of personality, most behavioral scientists agree that the personality of an individual is a useful predictor of behavior. Fortunately, unlike many of the other psychological concepts discussed in this book, factors defining an individual's personality are often observable. These include recurring patterns of specific behaviors which are called personality traits. These traits are the set of consistent responses which govern an individual's behavior and are frequently linked with deeply held values, attitudes, and beliefs.

Psychologists have identified many different personality traits. Personal appearance characteristics are perhaps the most obvious of these. Dress and grooming style often reveal much about an individual's personality. The use of certain products can also be related to personality traits. The kind of automobile, the consumption of certain foods, and the use of various consumer goods can all reflect the personality of an individual.

Psychologists have suggested paradigms or inclusive categorical descriptions of people based on personality. Many of these derive from psychoanalysis. Freud developed a personality typology based on his beliefs about infant sexuality and the manner in which this sexuality develops in the sexual behavior of mature adulthood. Freud argued that people pass through clearly marked phases in their sexual development and that fixation at any given stage will determine an entire set of personality characteristics which are manifested later in life. An individual who traverses a normal path of sexual development will arrive at what Freud described as the genital stage. Such a person will be interested in other people and the world outside himself. Much of his energy will be geared toward the attraction of people of the opposite sex, becoming socialized, joining groups, planning a career, getting married, and raising a family — all components of the so-called normal personality. Freud also felt that people who did not succeed in reaching the genital stage were neurotic in various ways. These people may be compulsive, narcissistic, overly aggressive, and competitive. They may also display tendencies to be sloppy and disorganized or compulsively neat.

There have been many attempts to derive other explanations of personality from Freud's basic ideas. One well-known typology posits that the predominant personality of an individual can be associated with one of three general categories. These personality traits are described as *aggressive, compliant,* or *detached.* Aggressive people are motivated to move against other people and to dominate and control their environment. Compliant people move toward or with others; they tend to acquiesce to social influence. Detached people move away from others and engage in avoidance behavior. Underlying the somewhat superficial characteristics of personal appearance and the use of certain products, one can often discern less obvious and perhaps more abstract characteristics of a juror's personality. For this reason, it is often valuable to inquire into a broad range of behaviors that may range beyond the immediate scope of the case when constructing juror personality profiles.

Personality, then, can be employed as an intervening variable in the assessment of jurors. By carefully observing the overt behavior of a person, personality structures can be inferred. These inferred characteristics may be compared to personality inventories contained in juror profiles or previously found through pretrial research to be associated with significant issues in the case.

## § 7-2(F). What About Demographics?

Generalizations concerning the demographic characteristics of jurors have not been promising. In fact, in the Litigation Sciences database consisting of over 14,000 juror interviews, demographic predictors of verdicts and of damage awards have, with one exception, consistently failed to be statistically significant. The only variable for which positive correlations have occurred relates to the sex of the juror: female jurors are more likely than males to award punitive damages. Hence, all of the juror stereotypes relating to race, occupation, and physical appearance should be viewed with great caution. They have simply not been borne out in the reality of repeated inquiry with large samples throughout the country.

### § 7-3. The Jury as a Social Group.

In addition to the characteristics that jurors display as individuals, trial lawyers must evaluate the individual's potential interaction with other members of the jury panel. Thus, a person may possess attributes which would ordinarily disqualify him as a desirable candidate but nevertheless be acceptable because of potential social group influences; and, of course, the opposite may be the case.

Group processes represent more than an aggregation or collection of individual behaviors acting together. Individual traits, when combined with those of others, may become exaggerated or modified. Hence, groups frequently become more or less than the sum of their parts. Group behavior is unique.

First time jurors are literally "strangers in a strange land." The pressures of a new environment where the rules governing behavior are unique, formal, and associated with an unfamiliar vernacular frequently place jurors in an atmosphere of stress and uncertainty. In such an environment, group identity and mutual support can become very important to the individual. Group identity is strengthened by juror interaction during the course of the trial. These interactions facilitate the formation of group norms as well as the development of negative and positive affiliations toward other members of the panel.

An important part of the decision-making process is that jurors learn early in the proceedings where their colleagues stand. Without discussion, they learn the position of other jurors through patterns of social influence, verbal and nonverbal cueing, and the formation of subgroups. The social interaction that leads to group formation, in fact, is one of the most important aspects of any jury. The formation of subgroups is also a preparation for the action of convincing others. Those who hold a particular position seek to build a network and set of defenses early in the trial. This is useful in anticipated confrontations over the verdict. Subgroups will thus consist of people who think alike and who have the same understanding about how they will carry out their roles as jurors.

Jurors are in an artificial, closely controlled environment, which precludes them from interacting in the very areas that, to them, are of social significance. They are jurors, but the very business of being jurors is just what they are not allowed to discuss.

Perhaps this can be more clearly understood through an analogy. Suppose that a group of employees were told that they could discuss anything among themselves except their job, their work environment, what they were doing, how they were doing it, and how their thoughts, observations, or opinions impacted upon them or the organization for which they worked. It is obvious that such a social environment would produce a great deal of stress.

The need to form subgroups seems to stem from two sources: a desire for interpersonal communality and the anticipation of who will be who vis-à-vis the verdict. Post-trial interviews with jurors who served on the CalComp v. IBM trial demonstrated the tremendous importance of subgroup formation. While IBM received a directed verdict after plaintiff's case-in-chief, post-trial interviews revealed that before the defense began its case, three distinct groups had formed: the pro-IBM group, the pro-CalComp group, and the group of the unannounced. Each group formed around a strong opinion leader.

The IBM group was led by a woman who was a doctrinaire believer in free enterprise. She and her husband regularly read the Wall Street Journal and together maintained a small portfolio of stocks they carefully tended. They followed an ultra-conservative lifestyle, and she, in particular, was a dogmatic and opinionated person who served as a kind of Pied Piper for this group. They clustered around her and through her found support and protection for their point of view. This group was educationally oriented and interested in current events, economics, and political issues. Thinking of themselves as philosophers, they were condescending toward the pro-CalComp group, whom they considered to be their intellectual inferiors and generally ill-informed.

The pro-CalComp group tended to form in reaction to the pro-IBM group and was much less pro-active. Its focal person was a woman who worked in a factory. She had a high school education, was very religious, and tended to be opinionated. She also disliked IBM and its lawyers intensely.

The third group, the unannounced, was made up of those who, although they were probably committed to one side or the other, did not announce their predispositions through any sort of signaling as to how they would have voted. In many ways, this group provided a major source of cohesion for the jury as a whole. Their position made them the conduit through which cooperation and negotiation would have to flow. The unannounced group would have played an important role in shaping group identity and in arriving at a verdict had the case gone to the jury.

Interviews also indicated that the jury foreman would have come from the unannounced subgroup. This individual was a 40-year-old construction foreman employed by the state of California who was particularly well-qualified for the role of foreman in this case. He was a mature male, strong without being aggressive, and a person who could take charge. He was a facilitator, pleasant, thoughtful, and trustworthy.

Subgroups among jurors can be seen in seating arrangements around a jury table, in car pooling, and in who goes to lunch with whom. They also are marked by the use of "safe talk." Since jurors cannot talk about the reason for their collective existence as jurors (the trial and their role in it), they invent safe topics which become the central thrust of their interaction in small subgroups. These frequently include common interests, work, sports, politics, hobbies, families, neighborhoods, and other mutual concerns. This use of safe talk is a frequent occurrence in juries. Safe talk enables jurors to find significant others, that is, people like themselves, and allows posturing and the formation of alliances.

The most typical safe topic used in the IBM case, as well as in many others, was food. Women brought in cakes, pies, cookies, and rolls. Inevitably, this became competitive. In other cases, when there are no men on the jury, women frequently bring food to the judge and the bailiff.

Among the people in the pro-CalComp group, food was the most frequent topic of safe conversation. The members of the pro-IBM group regarded the CalComp group as silly and intellectually deficient. They, in turn, considered the woman who led the pro-IBM group as "phony" and having unjustified intellectual pretensions.

Talk among members of the pro-IBM group was mainly about politics and current events. Members of this group spent much of their time sitting at their end of the jury table in their appointed places discussing these safe topics.

The moderates, or the group of the unannounced, centered on sports as their principal topic of safe talk. They saw the woman who led the IBM group as dogmatic and opinionated, but they did not necessarily dislike her. From the point of view of the IBM group, the group of the unannounced, with its talk of sports, was clearly inferior and plebian.

## § 7-3(A). Juror Roles.

All groups undergo a process of socialization. From the time a group forms until it disbands, it functions like a society in miniature. The major social process which takes place within a group is the formation of roles. The roles jurors play are related to the function of the jury as a group: to reach a verdict. Initially, jurors play the role of observers and investigators. Shortly after deliberation begins, they begin to shift into the role of persuader and decision maker. At this point, their roles may become adversarial.

The most important role that a juror can play is that of the opinion leader. One of the objectives of juror research is to identify people who are likely to become leaders and to determine the kind of influence they will exert on the rest of the group. The cluster of traits which seem to determine opinion leadership among jurors includes: a strong drive for responsibility and task completion; persistence and vigor in pursuit of goals; venturesomeness and creativity in problem solving; self-confidence; and a drive to exercise initiative in social situations. Leaders are willing to drive decisions forward, to absorb stress, and to accept the consequences of the decisions they make and actions they carry out.

The juror foreman may or may not be the group opinion leader. While the foreman is the titular leader of the group, he may merely carry out certain formal tasks. Indeed, the jury foreman may exert very little influence on the ultimate verdict. Oftentimes trial lawyers express a great deal of interest in predictions about which person will become the foreman of the jury. In reality, this may be misplaced attention. The real focus of attention in juror selection from a sociological perspective should be the identification of potential opinion leaders. Recognizing the opinion leader is a matter of carefully analyzing the past experience and background of jurors and attempting to discover which jurors have played the role of opinion leaders in other walks of life. It also includes an evaluation of those who display the capacity to lead vis-à-vis the composition of other people on the panel.

Juries work because not everyone wants to be a leader. Many people feel more comfortable playing the role of followers and facilitators. People normally defer to others who have greater ego-strength, greater skills, or higher intelligence. Jurors may also defer to other people they like. Liking can produce deference, as can fear. What kind of people are likely to defer to others and become followers instead of leaders? Followers can be identified in jury research by looking for certain traits and motivations such as the ones discussed earlier in this chapter. Jurors who conform easily, move toward people, and who have strong need to give and receive affection are likely to be followers.

### § 7-3(B). Personal Influence: How Leadership Works.

People will defer to others they consider significant in their lives. These can be athletes, teachers, religious leaders, media stars, or anyone else who seems to embody some ideal or provide information which can be used as a basis for decisions and actions.

People also can defer to others because of the perception that some individual is in a unique position "to know" through special training, education, or experience. The opinion leader may, in fact, possess none of these special attributes, but the perception that he does in comparison to other people in the group may propel him into a leadership position.

We create opinion leaders because we need them. Leaders on juries owe their leadership position to their ability to help other jurors accomplish the task at hand. Leaders initiate structure. They state the issues, organize what is taking place, and move the group toward its goal of rendering a verdict. This leadership may be exercised with moral suasion, fear, affection, or logical argument, but the ultimate task of the leader is to drive the group to accomplish its stated formal role.

### § 7-3(C). Personal Influence and Communication on the Jury.

Patterns of communication among jurors can be described as a series of networks. Significant issues or salient pieces of information during deliberations will be filtered in some way through other various members of the panel. Communication psychologists refer to this as a two-step flow of communication. When the jurors leave the courtroom to begin deliberations, they have not yet talked to each other about the case. When they do begin to discuss the trial, different jurors will remember different things and place differing interpretations on what they remember. The interpretations of some jurors will become a source of information for others. Strong-willed, dominant people with the best recall will generally contribute the most to this information recall process. People who become the most frequent sources of information on the jury will have the most personal influence. They will tend to become leaders and to steer the group process. This will also tend to become circular and self-fulfilling. Those who have the most information will gain personal influence and, as they gain personal influence, they will become more and more important as sources of information for other jurors.

If the trial lawyer can determine which jurors are likely to perform this role, special attention can and should be devoted to them during the course of the trial. This can include various forms of nonverbal communication as well as efforts to insure that charts, graphs, and demonstrative exhibits are clearly visible to these jurors.

## § 7-4. Conclusions.

This chapter has discussed a number of behavioral considerations which go into juror selection strategy which can be employed to complement lawyer instincts and intuitions. Well-designed juror selection strategies begin with lawyer instincts which are then juxtaposed to the insights and findings of pretrial juror research.

Juror selection strategies can be assisted by a number of concepts and principles from the behavioral sciences. These include a broad range of individual juror characteristics as well as the probable group process that will occur once the jury has been chosen.

Individual or psychological characteristics include patterns of motivation among jurors which will provide insights as to how jurors will regard the issues and participants in the trial. Although behavioral scientists are not in complete agreement about theories of motivation, all concur that people possess certain basic needs and are driven to gratify these needs. The way in which needs are disposed and gratified constitutes an individual's motivational pattern. Juror research strategy seeks, in part, to learn how motivational patterns will influence a juror's behavior in a given case.

Personality characteristics also influence juror behavior. Social psychologists have established the existence of a wide variety of personality traits which are found to be repeatedly associated with specific behaviors. Pretrial research can also be employed to demonstrate connections between juror behavior and these personality traits in a given case.

The second major area in which the behavioral sciences can contribute to juror selection strategy is in understanding the jury as a social group. Group identity and the way in which subgroups form within a jury is evident in many trials. This can be seen through the emergence of opinion leaders and through the observation of patterns of association, avoidance, agreement, disagreement, deference, and even conflict among members of the panel. Evaluations of how these patterns will occur and who will be likely to emerge as opinion leaders is an important aspect of selection strategy.

A final and important point about juror selection strategy is that pretrial research must be case specific. Every case is unique, and research must be oriented toward this uniqueness. The jurors, the courtroom events, the trial participants, the venue, and the issues which will be raised during the proceeding will constitute a one time only occurrence. It is most hazardous to suppose that the results of jury selection research conducted for one trial can be applied in an unqualified way to another. The carry-over which can be reasonably expected from one trial to another consists of testing propositions about jurors which may have worked once to see if they will work again. To assume that they will work again without testing them in the new setting is improper from a scientific standpoint and potentially dangerous to the client.

# CHAPTER 8

## OPENING STATEMENT STRATEGY



The beginning of the trial is the occasion when jurors are most attentive to the judge, lawyers, and courtroom events. They have not become conditioned to their new role, and the experience of being jurors is still novel and stimulating. As we have seen in previous chapters of this book, this is also the time when jurors possess the tendency to focus on and remember a great deal more of what is presented to them than at any other time during the trial. All of this, then, points to the great strategic importance of the lawyer's initial presentation of his case to the jury. In terms of helping shape the ultimate verdict, the opening statement is the most critical address an attorney will deliver during the trial. In fact, research on the impact of the opening statement consistently reveals that as many as 80 to 90 percent of all jurors have reached their ultimate verdict during or immediately after opening statements. Everything in the trial which follows will be selectively perceived to reinforce decisions which have already been made.

A good example of the importance of the opening statement occurred in the recent libel suit brought by Brown and Williamson against CBS. In a post-trial interview reported by *The American Lawyer,* the jury foreman stated that he and his cohorts were swayed early in the trial by the plaintiff's "rigorous" opening statement which contrasted sharply with the defendant's which he described as "flimsy."

The problems involved in composing an opening statement really focus on identifying which specific issues, among all of the possible alternatives, jurors must hear at the beginning of the case.

As we have seen, attorneys and jurors may not approach a trial from the same perspective. Jurors may focus on issues or concepts without the most legal relevance, or even without any legal relevance at all. These salient points may represent factual issues in the case or some highly perceptible emotional issue which will have a particularly persuasive impact.

In a recent product liability case, a child had suffered brain damage *in utero.* The plaintiff alleged that a drug manufactured by a large pharmaceutical company to induce labor in pregnancy was the cause of the defect. It was further alleged that the company had received indications of adverse reactions from physicians treating other patients. Clearly, these were serious allegations for the company.

In this instance, the case was settled before the jurors had completed their deliberations. Our pretrial research, however, had revealed an issue that would have been invaluable to the defense had the case gone to judgment. Utilizing excerpts of the mother's videotaped deposition, surrogate jurors were provided with key portions of the plaintiff's testimony. After observing the tape, the jurors were all deeply disturbed by their perception of the mother's apparent lack of love for the child. This fact, a negative attitude toward the plaintiff based on natural instincts toward children, did not refute any of the plaintiff's evidence. It was hardly a legal point and was not even in dispute. Nevertheless, this attitude, disapproval of the mother's apparent lack of love for her child, could have proved critical had the case gone to a jury verdict. It was completely inconsistent with the common sense belief that mothers should love their children under all circumstances. In this case, the relationship between the mother and the child would have been an issue of paramount importance. It would have allowed jurors to bring common sense to bear on the case, and using common sense is what most jurors are inclined to do. As such, this extra-legal issue, the mother/child relationship, was selected to be one of the central themes of the defendant's opening statement.

Throughout this book we have referred to these key issues or key concepts as Psychological Anchors.

## § 8-1. Psychological Anchors.

At Litigation Sciences, we have conducted hundreds of post-trial interviews with jurors and thousands of hours of pretrial research on behalf of our clients. The results of this work consistently reveal that jurors normally base their verdict on a small number of critical points. These Psychological Anchors represent the two, three, no more than four central themes or issues which support the overall theory of the case. Lawyers may call these "case issues," "case concepts," "theories of the case," or "case touchstones." Whatever the terminology, they are the deductive framework jurors formulate early in the trial and use to organize all subsequent details. These Anchors provide answers to nagging questions and are used to tie together loose ends and resolve lingering doubts.

If the jury remembers nothing else during the trial, hopefully they will remember the lawyer's Psychological Anchors.

Going into a trial, lawyers should be aware of what these Anchors will be since they will, in all likelihood, form the foundation of the jury's ultimate verdict. In most trials there are a variety of issues which can be presented. In one antitrust action, there were more than 400 individual issues which could be used to develop a theory of the case. In such instances, it is necessary to identify the three or four most important points on which the action will rest or fall. All of the evidence, testimony, lawyer argument, and significant demonstrative exhibits should relate to and reinforce these Psychological Anchors. If properly selected and employed, they tie together lawyer arguments, testimony, and demonstrative evidence.

Psychological Anchors exist in two forms. First, they are descriptive and represent matters of fact: things about which documents are written, witnesses testify, and exhibits present or explain. Factual anchors are the ones with which there is no dispute — the bridge collapsed, the plaintiff was injured, the bond default occurred. Reasonable people may argue over the cause or the consequences of an event, but descriptive anchors are rarely open to dispute.

It is interesting to note that descriptive anchors are the ones with which many lawyers feel most comfortable. Oftentimes, however, they are the least important to jury verdicts.

The second form of Psychological Anchors relates to matters of evaluation. These anchors are based upon the cognitions jurors carry with them into the courtroom. In a contraception product liability case, for example, issues relating to God, children, femininity, sexuality, motherhood, family, abortion, and death may be infinitely more important in verdict determination than testimony involving epidemiology, biochemistry, or arcane aspects of medical science. The legal, technical, or scientific facts of the case will evoke evaluative beliefs. If the trial lawyer fails to provide the jury with appropriate evaluative anchors, the jurors will employ their own. Without contributing strategic guidance in this "issue identification/issue selection" process, jurors may well focus on aspects of the case quite distinct and apart from the lawyer's intent.

## § 8-1(A). What Anchors Do for Jurors.

Psychological Anchors do several things for jurors. As we have noted, they enable jurors to organize the case consistent with their attitudes and beliefs. They also tend to provide jurors with a feeling of completion and security. They give jurors the rationalizations they need to settle the case in their own minds without lingering inner conflicts.

When jurors render verdicts, they have to make judgments and evaluations. Psychologists know that when people are asked to make judgments, they seek reference points around which to anchor these judgments. Evaluations and judgments are not made in a void. They are made with reference to an initially consistent and comfortable framework. This framework is the familiar one of cognitive structure or attitude set. When jurors are confronted with information which is hard to reconcile with fundamental beliefs and attitudes, they frequently experience a condition referred to as cognitive dissonance.

Cognitive dissonance consists of feelings of discomfort and even anxiety. The cognitive dissonance jurors sometimes experience when confronted with hard to digest information, not consistent with what they believe to be true, can be very uncomfortable. It can even produce states of acute tension and psychological disequilibrium. To avoid this psychological tension or dissonance, jurors, like people in other decision-making situations, will engage in a variety of coping mechanisms. These include: (1) rejecting the dissonance inducing information; (2) distorting the information to make it consistent with previously held beliefs; (3) minimizing the importance of the new information; or (4) changing their original beliefs or cognitive structure. From the lawyer's perspective, the last condition is probably the most logical. However, it is incredibly difficult to change most centrally held beliefs by merely presenting people with new information. As an example, the beliefs that most jurors hold relating to sexuality, religion, interpersonal relations, concepts of right or wrong or fair play, political orientation, or economic risk are relatively immutable. These belief structures are typically very resistant to change. Lawyer arguments, witness testimony, or judges' instructions which assault these cognitions or are inconsistent with them are likely to produce cognitive dissonance.

The kind of general stress under which jurors labor is only compounded by cognitive dissonance. Jurors are in unfamiliar surroundings. They are strangers in a world in which the attorneys and the judge are at home. Yet they are being asked to shoulder responsibility for allocating blame and possibly awarding large sums of money. Under these circumstances, jurors seek to reduce cognitive dissonance by screening out dissonant information.

### § 8-1(B). Implicational Molecules.

When confronted with a large amount of information, jurors will normally attempt to reduce it to what psychologists call implicational molecules. These are sets of statements which, when taken together, are cognitively consistent. When an implicational molecule or set of statements is inconsistent, it is eliminated.

Implicational molecules display three basic characteristics: (1) they tend toward completion; (2) once completed, they are resistant to change; and (3) when there are nonfitting elements, there is pressure to eliminate or correct the inconsistency.

The existence of Psychological Anchors is consistent with the notion of implicational molecules. As the three or four key issues in the trial in the juror's mind, Psychological Anchors work like implicational molecules. They are closely related to basic attitudes, and they afford cognitive consistency.

We can now summarize the ways in which Psychological Anchors work:

1. Psychological Anchors work by linking the issues in the trial to basic attitudes and beliefs in the juror's mind.
2. Psychological Anchors work by enabling jurors to cope with psychological tension and cognitive dissonance.
3. Psychological Anchors work by offering jurors a clear and succinct way of selecting information, organizing information, and making judgments about the case based on anchor points and a frame of reference.

## § 8-2. Using Psychological Anchors.

The effectiveness of Psychological Anchors is dependent upon presenting them in a highly structured context. Both the message contained in the Anchor, and the context in which it is used, ought to be consistent with the basic attitudinal structure of the jury. Consequently, careful thought must go into positioning Psychological Anchors. In opening statements they should appear as an overt or direct statement rather than in the form of connotation or innuendo. To maximize their effectiveness, Anchors should be articulated as short, easy to remember mnemonics and presented with clarity and specificity. It is also sometimes possible to introduce them this way in voir dire. Anchors should be repeated throughout the trial whenever possible. All the evidence should be introduced in support of the Anchors, and testimony should harmonize with the Anchors and even emphasize their content. In closing arguments, attorneys can then point out how the Anchors provide a coherent view of the case.

At Litigation Sciences, we have explored the role of Psychological Anchors in a large number of jury trials. Anchors give a juror a way to organize and integrate the bits and pieces of information introduced and discussed during the trial — information which might otherwise be forgotten. For jurors who are confused, impatient, or fatigued, Anchors can be a useful thread of meaning in a labyrinth of information. For jurors who reason deductively, Anchors can key into preconceptions and provide an avenue to a desired conclusion. Typically, Anchors provide opinion leaders with the means to convert other jurors. Anchors can also give a positively disposed juror the means to hold out against other jurors when a hung jury might constitute a victory for a litigant. In addition, they provide another important function: for jurors already committed to a verdict decision, Anchors can become ammunition for converting others.

## § 8-3. Psychological Anchors: Two Case Studies.

We will conclude our discussion of Psychological Anchors with the presentation of two case studies. The first of these involved a serious personal injury. The second related to the use of Psychological Anchors in an antitrust case.

### § 8-3(A). The Case of the Blue Arm.

One of the most interesting and unique Psychological Anchors in the experience of Litigation Sciences' work with clients occurred in a swimming pool accident. In this matter, a young couple checked into a resort hotel and went into the swimming pool. The pool was in the shape of a tropical lagoon. There was a cocktail lounge behind a waterfall in the pool where one could sit in the water and drink. The husband swam away under the waterfall toward the bar, leaving his wife in three and a half feet of water.

Inexplicably, the wife then slipped beneath the surface of the pool. There was no panic, no thrashing, no cry for help, no apparent trauma. The plaintiff alleged that the woman was under the water for at least four minutes before she was pulled to the surface of the water by another guest. The defense argued it had been less than a minute. In any event, the woman had suffered serious brain damage due to oxygen deprivation.

When Litigation Sciences became involved on behalf of the defendant, the case was focused essentially on two issues. These were swimming pool safety and an area of psychology called human factors analysis. Swimming pool safety experts were arguing on both sides as to whether there should have been side depth markings with big black letters, safety ropes and lights, and the number of appropriate life guards. (The safety experts would have designed this pool to look like the lap pool at the YMCA, hardly the ambience for a resort vacation.) The human factors experts were conducting a spirited debate on what a lifeguard could reasonably have been expected to see at certain distances from the water, given wind conditions and the glare of the sun.

When we read the depositions in the case, we found that they contained one rather curious phenomenon. When the plaintiff was pulled from the water, her right arm was blue from wrist to shoulder. Everyone, the man who had pulled her from the water, the paramedics, the ambulance driver, all the witnesses, had noticed this fact.

We put various aspects of this case on video tape and played our tapes before surrogate jurors in carefully controlled experimental settings. Attitudes and reactions regarding a number of issues in the case were carefully measured and related to jurors' previous experiences and background characteristics. We were interested in what kind of people would respond in what kind of ways to these stimulus tapes. Again and again, there was only one issue of real interest to jurors — the blue arm. Jurors were not engaged in the least by the debate among the swimming pool experts. They remained unmoved by the issues raised by human factors analysts.

Based on this research, it was suggested that the blue arm become a Psychological Anchor. It was carefully positioned in the defendant's opening statement.

The jury brought in a defense verdict in this case after only a few hours deliberation. In post-trial interviews, we were told they had actually reached their verdict in twenty minutes and spent the rest of their time developing an hypothesis for the existence of the blue arm. We had presented them with a cause for the drowning, albeit a mysterious one that no one could really explain. Attorneys set the stage for this defense in their opening statement, and all the medical experts on both sides were asked casually about the blue arm on the assumption that they would respond in the trial as they had in their depositions. They testified that there was no medical or scientific explanation for the phenomenon.

In examining these witnesses, our attorneys relied on the fact that most of us, including those who serve on juries, have feelings of dependency upon the medical profession. Deep down, however, many of us do not have absolute confidence that doctors and scientists know everything there is to know about life and many of the subtleties of the human body. When jurors in this case heard famous physicians from famous places respond that they did not know what caused the blue arm, their attitudes toward scientific and medical omnipotence were simply reinforced. They were ready to conclude that the plaintiff must have had some pre-existing and unrecognized physiological problem which caused her to lose consciousness and slip beneath the surface of the water. The blue arm explained a number of incongruous facts. It explained why there was no thrashing or panic. It explained why there was no sign of trauma. It also explained why there were no cries for help. Jurors concluded, that, while tragic, the hotel could not be held responsible for the incident. Here was a case in which a fact, the blue arm, had been of no initial importance to attorneys, or to any of the expert medical witnesses, but was of critical importance to jurors.

The Blue Arm is an interesting example of a Psychological Anchor for another reason. It is a textbook example of the internal attribution process discussed earlier. The lady almost drowned because of something in her own physical constitution. In terms of co-variation thinking, the way the criterion of consensus worked was overwhelming. Implicitly, jurors considered other drownings and other drowning victims. Other drowning victims did not have blue arms. Other drowning victims evinced panic. In other drownings there was thrashing about in the pool. This was not a normal drowning. This woman was not a normal drowning victim.

## § 8-3(B). Psychological Anchors in an Antitrust Case.

Psychological Anchors can emanate from Juror Attitude Survey data as well as the analysis of deliberation groups made up of surrogate jurors. At times, Anchors are suggested by our psychological and/or sociological analysis of themes which recur during simulated jury deliberations. These may emerge out of unanswered questions directed at the opposing case or from weaknesses in one's own case which need to be aggressively confronted.

One of the most challenging cases faced by Litigation Sciences in developing Psychological Anchors involved the computer industry. A group of distributors filed suit against manufacturers of computer equipment for conspiring to fix prices in order to keep the costs of accessory components artificially high. Evidence in this case was ambiguous. While there was very little actual evidence of collusion among the defendants, their prices were suspiciously similar. In general, these prices were significantly higher than those charged by other suppliers of similar equipment.

Our initial research on behalf of the defendants consisted of a series of small group experimental projects. From this research, we had access to the pencil and paper responses of a large number of subjects and later the results of four surrogate juries.

In the early phases of the research, one issue raised by a large number of subjects was the *process* by which list prices were established. Jurors were curious about the ratio of labor to parts charges, how time was factored into costs, and how markups were employed to establish prices at various levels in the distribution system. As our staff observed the groups wrestling with these issues, we began to recognize the necessity of providing jurors with a metaphor of an equation or formula. Jurors needed a simple structure as a way of explaining how a complex set of variables were combined to determine a price. In follow-up studies, we discovered that presenting pricing as a function of formulas or equations was an effective way of simplifying the complex economic issues in this trial. The metaphor permitted jurors to focus on the mechanical aspects of price determination. Consequently, we recommended the following Anchor: "There are three or four commonly used pricing formulas in this industry." This Anchor directly addressed the weakness of our client's case — similar prices among the defendant companies. Moreover, by using the word "formula," we set up a psychological rationale through which jurors could accept the fact that several companies in the industry could arrive at similar prices without being in collusion with regard to certain product lines and similar equipment.

While the first Anchor was aimed at repairing the defendants' principal vulnerability in this case, the second reinforced their major strength. This strength was the fact that there was no actual evidence of collusion among the three firms involved. In analyzing the handwritten responses of our surrogate jurors to open-ended questions, a curious pattern was observed. Plaintiff-oriented jurors tended to deal with the issue of collusion in the abstract. They were quite willing to believe that corporate executives do indeed get together to further their goals and would certainly do so with respect to price. Defense-oriented jurors were looking for specific indications of collusive behavior. With this finding, we wanted to develop strategies to force plaintiff jurors to deal with the conspiracy issue in the concrete rather than in the abstract. And hence, we needed to focus the notion of conspiracy *definitionally* on specific behaviors. We wanted to force the plaintiff jurors to deal with the fact that there was no evidence of collusion in the case as a definitional condition for a verdict in opposition to their predispositions. At the same time, it was necessary to reinforce defense jurors' perceptions of conspiracy based on concrete behavior. Hence, we worded the Anchor: "People get together to conspire." The real value of this second Anchor was that it served as a constant reminder to the jury that the burden of proof that collusion had taken place was on the plaintiff and that the plaintiff would not be able to produce such proof. Jurors whose judgment would have been based on a conceptual abstraction were forced to confront factual reality.

## § 8-4. Learning, Memory, and Retention.

In many cases, jurors are required to learn new information, concepts, or ideas which are foreign to their education, background, training, or previous experience. Hence, the learning process and the concepts of memory and retention are a critical aspect of the development of effective trial strategy. How do people learn? What is the learning process? And how does learning relate to juror behavior? There are many forms of learning which reflect the various processes through which people seek to improve their adjustment to and control over their environment. Here, we are interested in how these learning processes relate to juror decision-making. Learning is one of the fundamental processes of human behavior and is certainly a basic part of the behavior that occurs in a courtroom. No other field of psychology has generated the volume or quality of empirical research as the study of learning. Learning theorists have isolated a number of steps in the learning process. At a fundamental level, these can be classified as drives, cues, response, and reinforcement. *Drives* are stimuli that motivate individuals to some *response* in an effort to satisfy the drive. The specific response chosen depends upon the *cues* existing in the person's environment. *Response* is the overt or internal reaction to cues which stimulates a particular drive. *Reinforcement* of the process occurs when the response is followed by satisfaction, that is, a reduction in drive tension. Hunger, for example, could be thought of as a drive. A cue in this particular example might represent an advertisement for a food product. The response represents the person's reactions to the cue within his environment, perhaps the purchase of the food item. Reinforcement would be the extent to which the person is rewarded — in this example, whether or not the food item represents a satisfying experience. When reinforcement happens, the probability of a response being duplicated is increased — *habit formation* occurs. However, if the response is not reinforced over time, the learned habit could cease — *extinction* occurs.

*Drives* are strong stimuli that impel action. They may exist within the individual or emanate from external sources. Whatever the source, drives represent a state of tension which calls for action. Psychologists believe that drives exist at two levels. The first is referred to as primary drives. These are based upon innate physiological needs such as thirst, hunger, pain avoidance, and sexual gratification. Secondary drives are learned rather than innate and are derived from the primary drives. Examples of these drives include the desire for money, fear, pride, rivalry, and cooperation. In a courtroom environment, a secondary drive might be an internal sense of satisfaction from gaining mastery over the technical information presented in a particular case or the drive to be cooperative in a deliberation context. In order to understand how learning is likely to take place for members of a jury, it is critically important to have some indication as to the nature of the drives which will ultimately propel the learning experience.

As indicated earlier, *cues* exist within the individual or the environment and can be considered the force which awakens, arouses, or stimulates a particular drive. Many parents have learned that when driving with children in the car, the sight of McDonald's "Golden Arches" can become a cue that arouses the need to reduce hunger. In the courtroom, cues may represent demonstrative exhibits, witness testimony or specific Psychological Anchors utilized by the attorney in his opening statement.

From time to time in post-trial interviews, jurors report that "all of the witnesses in the case tended to blend together." This phenomenon represents an important and frequently encountered problem with learning in a trial environment. When witnesses, exhibits, or documents tend to blend together, *generalization* has occurred. Generalization refers to the jurors' tendency to make the same learned response to similar cues. On the other hand, *discrimination* refers to the jurors' ability to selectively respond to similar cues. Clearly, lawyers want jurors to engage in *discrimination* as it relates to the more positive aspects of their case — that is, to be able to discriminate and distinguish one witness from another, documents from each other, and one important chart or graph from another. At the same time, the trial lawyer would hope that *cue generalization* would occur with respect to his adversary's case presentation. That is, witnesses blend together as well as a tendency to consider documents and exhibits as similar rather than distinct from each other.

*Reinforcement* may be thought of as a reward. It strengthens the relationship between the environmental cue and the response and may lead to a similar response the next time the drive occurs. Repeated reinforcement obviously would lead to the development of a habit, thereby making the decision process routine for the individual. This approach to learning is referred to as the stimulus-response model of learning. When a direct connective relationship exists between a stimulus and a response, learning is said to have occurred.

### § 8-4(A). Building Associations.

One of the simplest forms of learning involves establishment of associations between two or more separate stimuli. In the courtroom, associations may be built by the simple repetition of the plaintiff or defendant's name with some specific behavior. For example, the plaintiff in a personal injury case might continually refer to the defendant and "corporate greed." With this method, the plaintiff will attempt to build negative associations with the defendant. Using the same strategy, the defendant might continually refer to the plaintiff's "personal irresponsibility" in the presentation of his case. Examples of building successful associations between some idea or concept and an entity are frequently seen in the world of advertising and marketing. For example, Wendy's hamburgers have been associated with "Where's the Beef?", and for many years General Electric with "Progress is Our Most Important Product." In both psychology and advertising, studies have demonstrated the effectiveness of building associations because consumers and subjects in experimental studies do indeed learn them. It is interesting to note that any reader of this book over the age of 35 will probably remember the slogan, "LS/MFT" even though it has not been used in advertising in more than thirty years.

There are two principal methods for establishing associations. The first is referred to as Pavlovian or classical conditioning. In the conditioning process, a bell is rung every time a dog is given food. After a time, the dog salivates whenever a bell is rung even though the dog has not been provided with food. This shows the power of associating the bell with food over so many occasions that such an intrinsically meaningless noise can produce the same response (saliva) as the food itself. While this stimulus-response approach has been refined over the years, it represents the fundamental learning model of Pavlov's experimentation with dogs.

Do these laboratory experiments have any relevance to juror behavior in the courtroom? Consider the impact of a series of long and dull depositions. Once jurors "learn" that depositions are boring, this association is likely to be reproduced throughout the rest of the trial when jurors are confronted with deposition testimony. The affirmative use of Pavlovian or classical conditioning by a trial lawyer might be to have a physically attractive, humorous, or likable member of the trial team deal with depositions early on. Hopefully, the jurors would "learn" to associate their positive perceptions of this individual with the information the lawyer is attempting to present through depositions. As another example, very interesting or attractively designed demonstrative exhibits could be presented to the jury in the early phases of the trial. Once again, hopefully there will be a tendency for the jurors to "learn" to associate the utilization of exhibits with interesting testimony.

The phenomenon of associations in the learning process is of great importance to trial lawyers in many ways. Aside from attempting to build positive associations for the lawyer's theory of the case, it is important to remember that jurors bring associations with them into the courtroom. Many of these associations have been formed over time, are based upon intensive experience, and may be totally inconsistent with the lawyer's approach to the case. As an example, jurors in a particular community may have learned through personal experience that banks are not caring or sympathetic organizations. Yet in an employment discrimination case, a trial attorney may unwittingly attempt to present the bank as a caring and sympathetic employer in the courtroom. Similar examples occur with attorneys representing utility companies. Very frequently, there is the desire to present an image of the company during the trial as responsive and dependable. Yet the very jurors who are the recipients of this intended message have learned that this is simply not the case because of their prior associations as consumers.

People in our society have learned to associate specific attributes of other people with specific personal qualities and characteristics. This is particularly important to remember in the selection of expert witnesses. Demeanor, voice, accent, and as we have already seen, attire frequently have a very special and specific meaning to jurors. Expectations exist concerning expert witnesses in particular. College professors are expected to look like, act like, and speak like college professors. Bankers and financial experts are expected to appear in navy blue suits with white shirts and conservative ties. They are expected to manifest an aura of aloofness with precision and overtones of caution. Bankers are not expected to be like college professors, and college professors are not equated with the learned associations relating to bankers.

Lawyers, like psychologists, have regrettably encountered what are called false associations. It is not uncommon for jurors to associate the expert witnesses for one side of the case with the other party. To avoid the potentially devastating impact of false associations, repetition throughout the trial is important. With key witnesses or key facts, redundancy is a very important tactic. In fact, redundancy and repetition are essential to reinforce learning up to the point of building negative reinforcement and boredom for jurors.

## § 8-4(B). Reinforcement Techniques.

Psychologists consider reinforcement to be a central concept in the learning process. Generally, it is believed that the greater the reward or reinforcement an individual receives, the stronger the association or learning. Rewards for jurors can come in a number of interesting ways. Lawyers can reward jurors by presenting them with interesting information. Most people experience a sense of personal pride with the acquisition of new knowledge. This is particularly the case when the knowledge or information is considered socially relevant and not possessed by many other people. In these situations, jurors can develop an inner sense of self-satisfaction by having learned things that their colleagues, friends, or family members would like to know but do not. When the lawyer or his witnesses provide jurors with this experience, the juror can be said to have been rewarded. Another form of rewarding jurors stems from the lawyer's ability to satisfy curiosity. Human beings are innately curious. Establishing a problem or an unanswered scenario and later helping jurors arrive at a solution can be a rewarding experience. Jurors can also receive psychological reward by arriving at or being provided with answers to important questions. Unresolved issues and unanswered questions tend to produce psychological tension and frustration. The elimination of these conditions can function as reinforcement or reward. Finally, trial lawyers can reward jurors by the lawyer's performance in the courtroom. As an example, if the trial lawyer is direct, concise, and very precise in the conduct of his direct or cross-examination, jurors can be rewarded by this behavior in contrast to long, protracted, and unfocused examinations by the other side.

## § 8-4(C). Participation in the Learning Process.

A fundamental and thoroughly verified principle of learning is that active participation in the learning process increases the speed and amount of learning. The more a juror enters into the learning process in some way, the better he learns. For this reason, the lawyer may attempt to inject the juror more directly into the learning process by techniques such as providing jurors with exhibit books which they can review during recesses or at the end of the day. This can also be accomplished with physical sight inspections, representational models, or the ability to touch, feel, or physically contact important pieces of evidence. Demonstrative exhibits are particularly effective in injecting jurors into a more dynamic learning environment.

Most jurors intrinsically enjoy learning and report in post-trial interviews that the most rewarding aspect in their jury service related to the fact that they learned so many new and interesting things.

## § 8-4(D). Memory.

After learning has been accomplished, there remains the important matter of *remembering* the information that has been learned. Some schools of clinical thought hold that nothing is ever really forgotten but that the material in question is simply inaccessible to the conscious mind under normal conditions. Results from hypnosis and psychoanalysis tend to support this view. In the courtroom, we are primarily interested in knowing what information has been learned. Further and more important, the lawyer is concerned not only about what information has been learned but also the extent to which it can be recalled accurately over time.

## § 8-4(E). Retention and Forgetting.

The stability of learned material over time is defined as retention and the converse is forgetting. Forgetting is the tendency for learned associations to weaken over time because of non-use, rather than a lack of reinforcement. Hence, for jurors to remember significant events that occur in the courtroom, it is incumbent upon the lawyer to remind jurors frequently through repetition whenever possible. In advertising research, it has been found that one exposure to a message induced content recall in only 14 percent of the subjects. Similar studies have reported that up to seven exposures may be required to achieve accurate recall. Most psychologists regard repetition as a key to successful learning. Without repetition, there is a significant delay in learned responses over time.

In general, distribution of messages over time has been found to be superior to concentration of messages in a limited amount of time to maximize the learning process. Taking this conclusion at face value would suggest that:

- — Psychological Anchors should be repeated and reintroduced as frequently as possible throughout the trial by the lawyer;
- — Psychological Anchors should be repeated and represented to the jury whenever possible through witness testimony and demonstrative exhibits;
- — The conclusions or most important aspect of an individual witness's testimony should be reinforced throughout that witness's direct testimony as frequently as possible;
- — Witnesses should reinforce and review the testimony of those who precede them and, if possible, help set the stage for the important topics of those witnesses who are to follow;

— Demonstrative exhibits should be designed to repeat and represent the major issues in the case; and
— Careful attention should be devoted to demonstrative exhibits to ensure that repetition and redundancy are built in to exhibits in an attractive and appealing manner.

### § 8-4(F). Primacy-Recency.

There have been numerous studies over the past fifty years investigating the order effects of new information on memory and retention. The general conclusions from this research suggest that people have a tendency to remember information that is presented first or last in a series of information. Absent factors to refocus attention, there is a U-shaped curve for memory and retention of material that comes in the middle. When student subjects participating in learning experiments are presented with a long list of names, they can later typically remember the names that appeared at the beginning of the list and names that were contained at the end of the list. Rarely can they recall names emanating from the middle portion of the list unless there is some unique or distinctive quality about a specific name. Replicating these studies with numerical data, subjects are presented with long lists of numbers. Experimental findings reveal that, if subjects can remember any of the numbers at all, they tend to remember once again the numbers that appeared at the beginning of the list and those at the end. For this reason, names appearing on election ballots in many states are randomly ordered. There is a statistical probability of prevailing in an election merely because a candidate's name appears at the beginning or end of a list of people seeking a particular office.

The implications of these primacy-recency effects have important strategic considerations to trial lawyers. As with subjects in psychological experiments, jurors have a tendency to remember what comes early in the trial — the opening statement — and that which comes at the end. The middle may tend to fade or blur.

Because of primacy-recency effects, opening statements address a critically important requirement at the beginning of the trial. If properly designed and delivered, the opening statement will provide an informational superstructure for the jury. We know that jurors will not attend to all of the *information* presented to them during the trial — indeed they cannot. Hopefully, the lawyer's Psychological Anchors will be learned, remembered, and employed to tie together otherwise potentially disparate documents, evidence, and witness testimony.

## § 8-5. Conclusions.

Pretrial research consistently reveals that jurors evaluate information presented in opening statements as more probative and salient to their final determination of the case than information they receive at any other time during the trial. To insure that the opening statement given by the attorney is the same one received by the jury, trial lawyers can focus on four important attributes which characterize an effective opening statement:

1. A direct sense of organization.
2. Sensitivity to the characteristics of the jurors.
3. Attention to nonverbal cues.
4. A commitment to practice and rehearsal.

Typically, opening statements present arguments in a temporal or linear fashion. A series of events is related chronologically: "On January 3rd, some action took place; on February 15th, there was this response."

There are a number of approaches to the problem of organizing an opening statement which may be more effective. First, it may be useful to base the opening statement on a series of major themes in the case. Second, factual topics can be employed as a basis for organizing the statement. Third, previews can be given of key witness testimony to serve as an organizational format. Fourth, critical events can provide a skeleton for the opening statement and for the case as a whole. Finally, it is often possible for constellations of facts, not necessarily related in chronological order, to provide the content of an opening statement.

In all that we have said thus far about opening statements, sensitivity to the characteristics of the jurors has been implied. Juror profiles are the beginning of this sensitivity. These profiles developed through pretrial research efforts can be refined by psychological observations made during voir dire. They can also be supplemented by our knowledge of previous juries in the venue. Understanding the psychological and behavioral characteristics of jurors permits the attorney to not only fine-tune the specific level of his presentation but also to clearly focus on the most appropriate techniques of persuasion.

Throughout voir dire and the delivery of the opening statement, attorneys have an opportunity to gain instantaneous feedback from jurors in the form of nonverbal cues. Attorneys can be attentive to signs of discomfort. Some of the more obvious of these include nodding, fidgeting, doodling, and other indications that something is going awry in the communication process. Jurors may also display positive nonverbal feedback. Attentive looks, as well as note taking, may be positive indications that the jury is paying attention. These positive cues, however, are less reliable than negative ones. Jurors frequently use positive cues to conceal a negative or neutral inner reaction.

Two final points relating to effective opening statements are probably gratuitous but are nevertheless frequently forgotten. First, preparation and practicing delivery are two of the most valuable pretrial activities on which a lawyer can spend his time. Consequently, the opening statement should be rehearsed extensively and before a video camera whenever possible. Notwithstanding comments that practicing an opening statement intrudes upon valuable time that should be allocated to other things, or that the opening will appear rehearsed and lack spontaneity, truly effective speakers thoroughly practice and rehearse before any major presentation. The great communicators of our time, Churchill, Kennedy, and Reagan, are well known for fastidious preparation before any important communication effort.

The second point about effective opening statements is that most of them are too long! When confronted with long opening statements, jurors are likely to become stimulus overloaded, confused, and even possibly bored. Because of the limitation of the human attention span, lawyers simply begin to lose their jury after about 30 minutes. In all of the cases in which Litigation Sciences has been involved, we have not seen a case that necessitated more of the jury's initial attention than a short 20- to 30-minute opening. This includes cases involving highly sophisticated and complex scientific, technological, and financial issues.

# CHAPTER 9

# JURY RESEARCH: THE KEY TO EFFECTIVE STRATEGY



The key to the effective utilization of the concepts and principles offered in this book is valid and reliable information about prospective jurors. If, for example, a trial lawyer suspects that certain types of jurors may hold negative attitudes toward his client, he needs to know with as much specificity as possible: (1) whether or not these suspicions are correct; and (2) the nature of these negative attitudes and the intensity with which they are held. This chapter will be concerned with an overview of how juror research provides valid and reliable answers to these kinds of questions.*

## § 9-1. The Need for Scientific Rigor.

Behavioral sciences bring with them a complex and sophisticated method of research and analysis. These disciplines deal in information called data, experimental facts, or statistics. This information comes in a language of its own and in many instances is different from that of everyday discourse. For those not trained in social science methodology, this language requires interpretation, and in many instances translation, before it can be successfully incorporated into trial strategy.

The use of scientific methods of data collection, measurement, and analysis are not novel. Detailed and rigorous behavioral research has long been employed by advertisers and communications experts. Not only do they recognize the importance of this research, but they also make full use of its findings prior to making significant decisions. No responsible corporate executive would consider expending or placing at risk millions of dollars solely on the basis of prior experience, instinct, or advice from a colleague. Today, there are very few advertising or marketing executives who "read consumers" or know "what sells" without a great deal of pre-market research. This is particularly true for companies like Procter & Gamble, IBM, General Foods, and others with a reputation for continual success in the marketplace.

The quality and integrity of juror research is dependent upon the use of a number of scientific procedures involving

*For an in-depth treatment of jury research methodology, the reader is referred to: *Social Science Research Methods for Litigation,* Donald E. Vinson and Philip K. Anthony, The Michie Company, 1985.

measurement, data collection, and analysis. Without the proper application of these procedures, we may be correct in what we predict about a jury, or we may be wrong. We won't know until jurors return their verdict. The point is, no legitimate social scientist would hazard a guess as to what a jury might do were he to merely walk into a courtroom and impressionistically "pick a jury." Frequently, we see jury consultants with inadequate training label jurors with certain traits, characteristics, or propensities. There are even those who will, after "reading the jury," provide the lawyer with assessments of the panel's ultimate verdict and level of damages! While there is an abundance of these self-styled experts who will provide attorneys with *ad hoc*, on-the-spot advice, this guidance is, in reality, not at all superior to what an untrained secretary or paralegal might provide. Social scientists who have devoted their professional lives to understanding how people behave will not engage in speculation or guesswork of this nature. Subjective guesswork made in the courtroom is not a valid and reliable basis for the development of strategies based on attitude theory, causal attribution, perception, learning, and the range of other topics considered in this book. These concepts, and their use, require the development of information about jurors based on scientific methods.

## § 9-2. Validity and Reliability in Juror Research.

When conclusions are reached about jurors, it is important to know how valid these conclusions are. How do we know *what we think* about jurors is in fact correct? Suppose someone tells us that jurors will find a particular witness convincing. Is this a valid statement? Upon what is it based? How can its validity be tested? Suppose it is suggested that blue collar workers will be good jurors for the defense because they proved to be defense jurors some years ago in a slightly related case. Is this a reliable supposition? Was it really the fact that because jurors were predominantly blue collar workers the attorney received a defense verdict in the first trial? Or was it a more complex set of interacting factors? Is it reliable to generalize from one trial experience to another? How similar are the two trials, and are the same issues going to be employed by jurors as a basis for their decision?

When social scientists talk about validity, they mean the following: Is something we believe to be true, actually true? For example, is it valid to suppose that by observing a juror's age, race, sex, or employment history we can accurately predict how that juror will respond to specific witnesses, learn evidence, comprehend instructions, or ultimately vote?

In addition to concerns about validity, jury research must be reliable. Reliability relates to the consistency of what we know to be. Will attitudes which are highly salient in one case remain so in another? Is it reliable to use the same trial strategies in a series of "similar" cases? What may have been a valid approach in one case may not be reliable in another.

Obtaining validity and reliability in this sense is only possible through the use of scientific methodologies. Social scientists are very concerned about the concepts of validity and reliability any time they attempt to predict or explain human behavior.

To insure the validity and reliability of pretrial research, data about jurors must be carefully collected and measured. The analysis of this data must proceed along the lines set by established statistical models. Sampling procedures must be adhered to with rigor, and typical errors of measurement and analysis, which have been studied and catalogued by experts in methodology, must be avoided.

In order to be certain that research results are valid and reliable and can be successfully applied to a given case, it is necessary to make juror research highly specific. Knowledge that certain kinds of jurors were good for a case in Denver some years ago will not be an adequate basis for decisions regarding a new case in Boston. Specific witnesses must be tested, as well as specific demonstrative exhibits, opening arguments, and prospective juror types. This must be done within the actual venue or a venue closely matched to the actual trial site.

## § 9-3. The Concept of Causality in Juror Research.

Statements that one thing has caused another are commonplace. It is often alleged during a trial that some injury has a direct and specific cause. Attorneys frequently attempt to teach jurors that the alleged causality is grounded on casual and impressionistic assumptions rather than scientific assessments of fact. In juror research, the concept of causality must be employed in a highly restrictive manner. When it is said that a plaintiff verdict was caused by the jurors' conviction that the pharmaceutical product in question had been inadequately tested by the defendant, did the corporate testing program really *cause* the jurors to decide the case against the defendant? Could there have been another cause? Or more likely, could there have been a number of contributing factors ranging from other important facts to the trial lawyer's presentation of the case to the jury? While it may sound simplistic and naive, the staff at Litigation Sciences are frequently told that "a company witness lost the case," or that "the jury didn't understand the judge's instructions."

Since lawyers often exercise considerable efforts to educate jurors to the real meaning of causality, it is interesting that the concept is difficult to apply in the case of understanding jurors and the decisions they make. Social science experts do not lightly assume that a given trait or set of traits can "cause" jurors to decide a case one way or the other. It is far more valid to look for probable associations between a verdict on the one hand and some set of attitudes, traits, or demographic characteristics in the jury. In juror research, a search takes place for the way in which jurors display certain cognitions and behavioral intentions with regard to the facts in the case, the litigants themselves, or even the legal counsel involved. What jurors say about how they feel and what they think they will do is a complex tapestry. It must be studied very closely. Correlations and associations can be discovered which will be useful in predicting verdicts with a certain stated probability. This is far different from saying that one thing has caused or will cause another.

## § 9-4. Data Collection.

Data is the information we seek about jurors. It consists of juror demographic traits, such as education, occupation, residence, sex, age, and religion. It also includes information about juror attitudes and beliefs, juror verdict preferences, biases, and stated behavioral intentions with regard to the specific case under consideration. There are consequently many different kinds of data which take many different forms.

Data are collected to be measured, analyzed, and interpreted. The types of measurement, analysis, and interpretation which social scientists employ require that the data be collected in highly specific ways using what are referred to as measurement scales.

### § 9-4(A). Measurement Scales.

Most data collection in jury research is a matter of asking surrogate jurors (people matched to the general characteristics of the anticipated panel) questions or by observing their behavior. These questions must be designed to yield specific structured responses so that the resulting data will be valid and reliable. Data are generally numbers or verbal responses translated into numbers. It is important to be able to put these responses into numerical forms so that statistical analysis can be employed to interpret their meaning.

In our everyday lives, we tend to think about measurement in the sense of well-defined scales having a natural zero point and constant unit of measurement. At one time or another, we have found it useful or necessary to use measuring instruments such as yardsticks, gasoline gauges, and weighing scales to determine such things as height, volume, and weight.

In behavioral research, there are various types of scales which are based on the underlying assumptions regarding the correspondence of numbers to the properties of behavior and the ability of performing mathematical and statistical operations on these numbers. While there are many data classifications schemes, the most appropriate for our discussion in this book are referred to as *nominal, ordinal, interval,* and *ratio* scales. Each of these possesses very specific properties and is related to specific standards of empirical analysis.

*Nominal scales* consist simply of classifying objects, events, individuals, or behaviors into categories. Each category is given a name or assigned a number. These names or numbers are used merely as designations or labels. Nothing else is inferred; there is no implied relationship among the numbered categories. With respect to religion, for example, jurors could be classified as:

1 = Protestant
2 = Catholic

3 = Jew
4 = Other

With nominal scales, there is no qualitative or quantitative assessment given to the scaled categories. In this example, the Protestant rating is not "higher" or "lower" than any of the other classifications. Because the numbers assigned to categories making up a nominal scale serve only as tags or labels, arithmetic calculations performed on nominal data have no meaning whatsoever. For example, one cannot calculate a mean average of nominal data. Hence, there are severe limitations associated with the statistical analysis of classification scales.

Another kind of useful scale is called an *ordinal scale.* Ordinal scales place categories in some order with respect to the degree to which each category possesses some characteristic or trait. Yet we cannot say in numerical form how much this is. An example will make this clear. Suppose we wish to know how believable prospective jurors consider certain product testing organizations. We might ask jurors to use an ordinal scale to rank a number of different organizations and then obtain data in this form:

| | |
|---|---|
| Most believable | 1. Consumer product testing agencies. |
| | 2. University Research Centers. |
| | 3. Independent testing laboratories. |
| Least believable | 4. Manufacturers' testing programs. |

Here, an ordinal scale, or ranking scale, has been employed to indicate the extent to which these agencies possess an intangible quality called believability. The categories are placed in order or rank according to the central characteristic which is being tested. Ordinal data present more information than data from a nominal scale but still do not allow meaningful use of arithmetic operations.

*Interval scales* are another form in which behavioral data are frequently collected. An interval scale has all the characteristics of ordinal measures, and, in addition, the units or intervals between successive positions are equal. For this reason, these scales or attempts at creating them are particularly important in juror research. Many of the constructs discussed in this book such as attitudes, learning, and perception are measured with scales containing equal-appearing psychological intervals. As an example, the perceived competence of an expert witness can be measured on an interval scale from +5 (very competent) to -5 (very incompetent). Because a mean average and standard deviation can be calculated from interval data, very sophisticated statistical analysis can be performed.

Finally, *ratio scales* may be used in juror research. With these scales, a ratio of numbers is used to express the degree to which some attribute is possessed. Ratio scales are often very useful in presenting data. Suppose that in a given venue, 80 percent of the prospective jurors have a direct economic interest in the outcome of a public utilities case. It might be useful to state that the ratio of potentially biased jurors in this case is 4 to 1. Ratios can also be used to indicate rates. It might be important to note that the accident rate at a particular intersection is 612 per hundred thousand vehicles and that the average for 10 other intersections in the same part of town is only 52. Thus, there is an almost 12-1 greater chance of having an accident in the first intersection than in any of the others. All parametric and non-parametric statistical procedures may be undertaken with ratio-scaled data, and hence ratio data provide maximum flexibility in data analysis.

Ratio scales are found more commonly in the physical sciences than in the behavioral sciences. Measures of weight, length, time intervals, velocity, etc., all conform to ratio scales. In the social sciences, we do find some variables such as money, age, and years of education which can be ratio scaled.

## § 9-4(B). The Likert Scale.

One commonly used form of questioning in jury research is referred to as a modified Likert Scale. A Likert Scale is a rating scale with response categories ordered to represent the degree of a respondent's agreement or disagreement with a statement. This can be illustrated by the following:

| "How do you feel about radial tires?" | | | | | |
|---|---|---|---|---|---|
| | Strongly Agree | Agree | Neither agree nor disagree | Dis-agree | Strongly disagree |
| Bias ply tires are not as safe as radial tires | | | | | |
| Radial tires should be required by law | | | | | |
| People who do not use radial tires should pay higher insurance pre-miums | | | | | |

People can be asked to indicate the extent to which they agree or disagree with these statements. There are other ways to ask these questions, but the use of a Likert Scale has the advantage of measuring not only agreement versus disagreement but the intensity with which an opinion is held.

### § 9-4(C). Questions Based on Semantic Differential Scales.

Another useful question form is the Semantic Differential Scale. Semantic Differential Scales are rating scales in which responses are ordered to evaluate an object on the basis of some bipolar attribute. Here is an example:

> Please indicate the degree to which you think the corporation is characterized by the following traits:
>
> Good Employer ............................ Bad Employer
> Large Company ........................ Small Company
> Responsible Firm ................... Irresponsible Firm

These bipolar adjectives or statements can be used to investigate the image of the plaintiff or the defendant, the salient attributes of a case presentation, or even to assess the characteristics of witnesses or demonstrative exhibits.

Obviously, the design of questionnaires and the questions they contain is both a subtle and an important aspect of jury research. One important application of this art is the design of questions for voir dire. Of course, research into juror attitudes and verdict preferences remains the primary and fundamental application of test instruments.

### § 9-4(D). Techniques of Data Collection.

There are a number of techniques which are useful in collecting juror research data. These include the use of either structured or unstructured interviewing procedures and a mix of direct and indirect approaches.

A structured interview is an interview made up of a series of highly specific questions to which there can only be one of a selected number of given responses. If a prospective juror is asked to classify himself as a liberal, moderate, or conservative, the question is specific, and the responses are structured as a series of three possible choices. It is also possible to inquire into political attitudes and preferences through the use of unstructured questions. A prospective juror could be asked: "What are your political preferences?" Now, the answer would probably be somewhat rambling and much less precise. Such an answer might, however, yield information which was not obtained through the use of a structured question.

Questioning procedures can be either direct or indirect. Usually, juror research uses a combination of both approaches. Direct questions inquire directly into the matter about which information is sought. If it is desirable to know what a prospective juror thinks about a particular corporation, a direct inquiry can be employed. The obvious problem in doing so is that the respondent may identify the interviewer as someone who has a special interest in the matter, either pro-company or anti-company, and give a biased response. Indirect questions, about a category of companies or companies with certain traits, will appear more objective to respondents. Thus, the information gained from indirect questioning may be more reliable. The point is that there are times when structured or unstructured interviews should be used and times when questioning should be either direct or indirect. The choice of data collection technique will have a significant impact on the quality of the data.

In many jury research applications, a test instrument or questionnaire is used. This will enable the investigators to treat each respondent exactly the same way and to accurately compare, for example, verdict preference with attitudes toward specific issues. By treating each respondent in precisely the same way, reliability can be assured.

Since the data collected through the use of the test instruments are subjected to sophisticated statistical analysis, it is necessary to gather this data in some convenient numerical form. This means that questions must be structured in such a way that the response leads logically to the assignment of a numerical value. The simplest way to do this will be to ask questions which have two-valued answers such as: Are you married? The answer will be "yes" or "no." Such an answer can be readily given a numerical form such as 1 for "yes" and 0 for "no."

A major limitation which must be taken into consideration when data collection procedures are used is that the questioning process itself may bias the response. Unskilled and untrained interviewers often obtain unreliable data because they are unaware of problems associated with validity and reliability. If a correct answer is embarrassing to a respondent, the response is likely to be disingenuous. Under some circumstances, respondents will give answers because they think such answers will be pleasing or acceptable to the person conducting the research, not because the answers represent the true state of their opinions. Data may also be unreliable because respondents are being asked for information they do not possess. Prospective jurors may have been told too little about a case, or given misleading information about it. If this occurs, their responses will not provide a reliable guide to the way in which they would actually behave if asked to serve on the jury.

## § 9-5. Juror Attitude Surveys.

Juror Attitude Surveys use a method of investigation called survey research, which is one of the most important means of data collection and analysis employed in the application of social science concepts to litigation. Survey research has been employed as a way of testing hypotheses in economics, sociology, political science, and marketing. It has been made possible by the development of procedures for selecting probability samples from large populations. It also requires techniques like the ones discussed above for obtaining valid and reliable information from a test population. Finally, survey research rests upon procedures of statistical analysis which can only be carried out in a cost efficient manner through the use of modern high speed computers.

In practice, survey research is the investigation of some area of concern in which people hold distinctive attitudes and beliefs. These attitudes and beliefs are ascertained through the development of carefully composed questions which constitute the survey instrument. Usually the number of questions is a compromise between the scope of the survey and the need to deal with respondent fatigue. The survey is then administered in person, through the mail, or by telephone. In jury research, telephone surveys are the most efficient and reliable. The survey will include questions about who the respondents are and the attitudes, experiences, and associations they have in relation to the case.

### § 9-5(A). Question Criteria.

The purpose of any questionnaire is to gather information. However, the way in which a questionnaire is designed will have a determining effect on the reliability of the data which is obtained. As the study of juror bias discussed in Chapter 4 demonstrates, the way in which questions are asked can have a tremendous impact on the ultimate findings of the study. There are a number of criteria which must be employed in the construction of questions for Juror Attitude Surveys. When these criteria are properly implemented, the quality of the information gathered in the survey is greatly enhanced. For any research instrument, considerations of economy should govern the asking of questions. Only questions which have direct value within the context of the survey's overall objective should be asked. Respondents will display only a limited amount of patience and cooperation in answering questions; this generally will not exceed 20 minutes.

Another criterion which must be employed in formulating questions concerns whether or not the items will actually elicit the desired information. A problem frequently encountered in jury research is that respondents have the information we want but they will not reveal it. For example, it may be important to know whether or not prospective jurors have used contraceptive products, have had cosmetic surgery, have ever defaulted on a loan, or have been responsible for the death or injury of another person. Yet these subjects are of such a nature that prospective jurors may be reluctant to disclose this information in the context of a survey. Nevertheless, these and other sensitive subject areas can be successfully explored when questions are properly framed and presented to the respondent. The design and formulation of research instruments dealing with these kinds of issues require a great deal of experience and sophisticated training in an area of psychology called psychometrics. Psychometrics involves the measurement of human responses utilizing advanced statistics and mathematics.

In the case of Juror Attitude Surveys, the content of the questions will be determined in large part by a process of applying common sense, intuition, and the appropriate social science theory. The matter of appropriate theory is very important. The content of questions regarding attitudes and behavior must be predicated on certain expectations regarding attitudes and behavior in the general population for us to discover. In the case of jury behavior, we must have some hypotheses about relevant behavior constructs and make these hypotheses part of our questions. These hypotheses will depend on past data, our experience with juror research in general, and our theoretical knowledge about how jurors work.

## § 9-5(B). Independent and Dependent Variables in Surveys.

Any research effort must specify what are called independent and dependent variables. This distinction is critical in designing Juror Attitude Surveys.

Independent variables, as the name implies, are independent of the characteristic or quality we are attempting to explain, predict, or estimate. In jury research, independent variables are the characteristics jurors possess at the beginning of the trial, like age, income, educational level, sex, occupation, personal experiences relevant to the issues in the case, and experience as consumers and members of society in general. Relatively immutable attitudes possessed by jurors are also independent variables.

Dependent variables are the specific behavior or reactions we want to predict or explain. Because juror research represents an effort to provide these assessments in a valid and reliable way, it is important to find out what kind of linkages exist between independent and dependent variables. It is important to gain clear and unambiguous information from Juror Attitude Surveys about both independent and dependent variables so that an analysis of potential juror perceptions, reactions, and verdict decisions can be undertaken.

## § 9-5(C). Basing Trial Strategy on Survey Research.

Numerous trial strategies can be based on survey research. The most obvious of these is juror selection *per se.* Attitude surveys can also be used to discover and confirm Psychological Anchors, or to evaluate the desirability of possible Psychological Anchors for use in the case presentation. In one antitrust case, for example, the lawyers felt that there were more than four hundred issues which could have been presented to a jury to prove that the defendant did indeed violate the antitrust laws. Research with small groups was employed to reduce this number to about ten. At this stage of the research program, survey research was then conducted to carry out a precise investigation into potential juror attitudes toward these ten issues. Based on the results of the survey, a relatively small number of issues, three or four in number, were seen as most central to the case. In this manner, it was possible to learn not only how jurors responded to these issues but also to evaluate the intensity of their relevance.

## § 9-5(D). Other Considerations.

*Change of Venue.* At times, the lawyer's judgment or pretrial research demonstrates the need to enter a motion for change of venue. Survey research into the sample of potential jurors may reveal the existence of intractable bias and a tendency to prejudge the case among such a large number of potential jurors that a cogent argument for moving the trial to another locale can be advanced.

*Post-Trial Analysis.* Post-trial analysis, including in-depth interviews with jurors, can often determine why a jury reached its verdict. The resulting information can then be applied to similar cases in the future and can assist with multi-district litigation.

## § 9-6. Small Group Research.

Small group research is based upon the proposition that a sample population can be studied in a context which closely simulates the actual environment in which the relevant behavior will occur. Studies of juror behavior focus on gaining an understanding of the characteristics the group displays in the course of doing its work. What social phenomena can we actually observe taking place? What do people say to each other, what kind of nonverbal cuing takes place? How do jurors orient themselves toward the task and toward each other? How do they positively and negatively sanction statements by others?

Small group methods are focused on delineating social phenomena and on describing factual reality with maximum precision. Variables which are generated by this delineation can then be operationally defined, scaled, and used in surveys or experiments to discover the causes of the behavior observed.

Small group research has a number of applications in the development of trial strategy. These include the identification of salient dependent and independent variables, the assessment of key witnesses, exhibits and documents, and the opportunity to evaluate competitive strategies and tactical alternatives. Small group analysis is, however, more sophisticated than simply throwing a group of people into a room to watch them talk. To be used correctly, it requires a great deal of in-depth training in sub-specialties of sociology referred to as phenomenology, ethnomethodology, and participant-observer research.

### § 9-6(A). Jury Simulation.

Another important application of behavioral science research methods to litigation is jury simulation. In jury simulation, unlike other kinds of small group research, a surrogate jury is presented with the actual case and asked to deliberate as if they were the real jury. Observing this deliberation process provides insight into how an attorney is communicating and how effective his trial strategy is going to be in court. In essence, a case can be won or lost on an experimental basis prior to its actually being heard before judge and jury.

## § 9-7. Experimental Designs.

The research product attorneys use in devising trial strategy can also be based on carefully thought out experiments. Experiments consist of forming hypotheses about some course of action and setting up a means of testing these hypotheses. Experimental designs have been employed to test chemical substances, ideas or concepts, and products from pharmaceuticals to automobiles. They can also be used to test aspects of an attorney's case. It might be hypothesized that opening statement A is superior to opening statement B. This hypothesis can then be tested in an experimental setting utilizing surrogate jurors as subjects. Experimental designs can also be employed to assist with decisions regarding alternative approaches to the use of demonstrative exhibits.

In a recent case, a manufacturer of light airplanes was alleged to have designed and built a defective plane that was not airworthy in certain take-off and landing conditions. The defense had at their disposal a number of ways of demonstrating to the jury that the aircraft was airworthy and could not have been defective in the way plaintiff asserted. There was an available film of the aircraft showing it taking off, performing in the air, and landing. Second, the defense had access to various models of the airplane which could be shown to jurors. Finally, the judge in this case was willing to permit jurors to go to a local airport to inspect and become acquainted with actual aircraft of the type in question.

It was important to know which of these kinds of evidence would be most useful, if useful at all, to the defendant. The dependent variable in this case was the jurors' reactions to each of these three different kinds of evidence. In order to ascertain what these reactions would be, an experiment was devised using what is called an *after-only* experimental design. In such a study, the jurors' reactions to the different kinds of evidence would be measured one time only, after their initial exposure to the treatment or independent variables. Matched groups of jurors were shown the film, shown the model, and taken to the hangar to look at the actual plane. The reactions of the jurors to the defense claim that the airplane was safe were then carefully measured. Those who had seen the film had relatively neutral reactions. The film didn't seem to hurt the defense, nor to help very much. The trip to the airport, however, proved very damaging to the defense. Jurors saw a washer on the ground beneath the plane, oil and grease stains on the tarmack, and other subtle things that actually heightened their level of flying apprehension. The airplane did not seem as substantial and solid to jurors as they had anticipated. In fact, the visit to the airport stimulated negative attitudes toward safety, small airplanes, and the airworthiness of this particular aircraft. The model, however, proved to be very positive and useful in supporting the claims of the defendant concerning the safety. The model was used in court and contributed significantly to a verdict for the defense.

In practice, the use of experimental methods can be rather complicated. Factorial designs, for example, are designs in which two or more variables are tested at the same time and in interaction with each other. Such a procedure can be used in juror selection research in which it is necessary to study the effects of many independent variables upon a potential juror's verdict preference. With factorial designs, it is possible to study what are called the "main effects" of a variable, as well as the effects of that variable interacting with others. The analysis of these designs can be highly complicated and dependent upon advanced training in mathematics and statistics.

There are many ways in which experimental designs can be misused. If, for example, the same group of jurors were shown each of the kinds of evidence considered in the airplane products case noted above, no valid research results could be obtained. The lack of validity in such a procedure would come from what is called the pretest effect. Having seen the film, study subjects would be sensitized to the topic of the lawsuit, and their reactions to the model would not be the same as if they were viewing the airplane for the first time. This is a matter of what is called internal validity, that is, measuring in fact what we think we are measuring. In Ph.D. seminars, psychologists and sociologists are concerned about the various threats to validity and the mathematical processes by which these threats can be controlled or eliminated.

## § 9-7(A). Generalizing Experimental Results.

In order to generalize from an experiment involving a number of potential jurors to the juror population as a whole, experiments must have what is called external validity. Jury research is aimed at providing reliable generalizations about all the jurors who may be called in a given case. As such, the jurors used in the research must be representative of this larger population. This quality of representativeness is what gives an experiment external validity.

### § 9-7(B). Reliability in Experimental Designs.

Finally, in order to insure reliability, an experiment needs to be repeated on different occasions and the results compared. If the research result can be replicated and the results do not vary across experiments, the findings can be taken to be reliable. Thus, although a design like the after-only design used in the airplane case may sound simple when summarized, this design must be employed with caution and knowledge for proper experimental research procedures. Otherwise, an invalid and unreliable research result can be obtained.

## § 9-8. Statistical Analysis.

In a number of places in this chapter, the concept of statistical analysis has been raised. Statistical analysis is designed to portray the relationships which exist among variables. These relationships are of several types, and various techniques of statistical analysis are needed to describe and discover each of these relationships. While there is a wide variety of statistical procedures available to help analyze juror research data, the method by which the data were collected and the form in which presented is of critical importance. In fact, untrained people frequently write questionnaires and collect data which are incompatible with meaningful analysis.

### § 9-8(A). Types of Statistical Analysis and the Form of the Data.

The topic of statistical analysis obviously exceeds the scope and intent of this book. In fact, people can devote their entire careers to the mathematical sophistication associated with research methodology. Hence, the intent here is to present the reader with an overview of some of the most frequently employed analysis procedures. These include:

*Analysis of variance* is a technique for showing the dependence of one or more metric variables upon one or more treatment or independent variables which are nominally scaled. By metric data, in this case, we mean interval scaled or numerical data.

*Regression* is a technique of statistical analysis for showing that the presence of one variable can be used to predict the presence of another. In order to use regression, all the variables must be metric, or intervally scaled. Using regression, it is possible to predict a juror's verdict on the basis of several characteristics. This prediction can be made with a stated probability.

*Correlation analysis* is a way of showing the strength of association between metric variables. The measure of association is summarized in a single number, and the magnitude of this number is a measure of the strength of this association. Thus, using correlation analysis, it is possible, for example, to state how strongly a juror's attitude on a certain subject will predict the juror's verdict.

*Discriminant analysis* is still another useful technique of statistical analysis. Discriminant analysis can be used when there are nominally scaled dependent variables like verdict preference, which is dichotomous or has two values — preference for the plaintiff or for the defendant. With this procedure, variables like juror age, level of education, and level of income must be metrically scaled. Discriminant analysis permits the grouping or clustering of those independent variables which best discriminate between jurors who favor the plaintiff and those who favor the defendant.

In addition to these procedures, there are a number of additional statistical analysis techniques which are frequently used in jury research. These include factor analysis, canonical correlation, multiple regression, and multidimensional scaling. Each requires a specific kind of data, and each can be used to show specific kinds of relationships among variables.

## § 9-8(B). Univariate, Bivariate, and Multivariate Techniques.

In addition to the desirability of a specific kind of analysis, statistical techniques also depend upon the number of variables to be considered. When the analysis consists of only a single variable, these univariate techniques are referred to as descriptive statistics. Descriptive statistics are employed to demonstrate the distribution of a variable (the ages or sex of a jury panel) or to provide measures of central tendency — the average age of the panel, the median level of income, etc.

Bivariate analysis refers to statistical analysis of two variables. This type of analysis would be infrequently encountered in research due to the complexity of juror decision making. It is difficult to envision a situation in which an attorney would be concerned about the impact of only one independent variable, say juror sex, and a dependent variable such as the credibility of a particular witness. Correlation and regression techniques are the primary types of statistical analysis used in bivariate models. When many variables are under consideration, it is customary to speak of multivariate analysis. Multiple regression and correlation, analysis of variance, multiple analysis of variance, discriminant analysis, and factor analysis are all used in multivariate models. With these procedures, it is possible to analyze any number of independent and dependent variables simultaneously.

## § 9-8(C). Sampling.

A thorough knowledge of sampling and sampling techniques is essential for the meaningful use of juror research in the development of trial strategy. Without adequate sampling procedures, research cannot be considered valid or reliable. It is, therefore, extremely hazardous to base any juror selection decision or trial strategy consideration upon research for which sampling procedures were not carefully designed and evaluated.

In jury research, prospective jurors in the venue are considered the basic population or sampling frame. To define this population, some list like a list of registered voters or the names of licensed drivers, in some jurisdictions, can be used. The premise of any sampling procedure is that the population can be sampled in such a way that the people chosen, although relatively small in number, will exhibit the same characteristics found in the entire population.

Sampling is really a commonsense procedure. Suppose a new film is opening and the producers wish to know if the ending is effective. Investigators can be hired to ask each person leaving the theater how they liked the ending. Using this procedure, not everyone in the theater will be sampled, however. Those who did not like the film and have left early would not have been encountered by the interviewers. Shy people may also avoid the investigators. Even though a sample will have been taken, how reliable will it be? And even if it is a reliable indicator of how the film plays before this particular audience, will their response be representative of an audience in another city? Obviously, this approach will not suffice for more than an initial, and not very reliable, impression.

In order to insure that the statistics of the sample have a high probability of actually representing the population, it is necessary to take a random sample. A random sample means that each member of the population has a chance of being included in the sample which is equal to their proportional membership in the population. If half the population is Catholic, then Catholics should have a 50-50 probability of being included in the sample. If 1 in 5 people in the population is a married woman, then every married woman should have a 20 percent chance of being included in the sample. If the sample is made up in such a way that 75 percent of those interviewed are Catholic and 50 percent are married women, it is not a random sample, and the statistics provided by the sample will not be reliably representative of the population as a whole.

The laws of statistics tell us that if a sample is randomly selected and of sufficient size, the statistics in the sample will reflect the actual characteristics of the population. In practice, there will be some error in any statistical procedure, most of which will be sampling error. However, the rules of statistical sampling will tell us how great this error is. Statisticians use the term confidence interval to describe how likely our statistics represent actual population parameters. A 95 percent confidence interval is commonly achieved. This means that it is 95 percent certain that sample statistics represent the population parameters or characteristics.

Choosing the correct sample size in jury research depends upon several factors. These are the confidence level we wish to achieve and some reasonable estimate of what we expect the population parameters to be. With complex research designs, calculating these factors properly is a task for expert statisticians.

Advanced knowledge of statistics becomes even more essential in research involving small groups. Here, non-probability samples must be utilized. The technical reason for this is that the law of large numbers does not apply to small samples, and it cannot be assumed that all the traits under study are normally distributed in the population. While it would be beyond the scope of this book to explain these concepts, this area of statistics is referred to as non-parametric statistics. The point to be made is that statistical analysis is often valuable in small group research but that it is difficult to do and can easily generate totally meaningless results if the proper techniques and safeguards are not employed.

## § 9-9. Conclusions.

It has been said at the outset of this chapter that jury research is the key to effective jury trial strategy. Furthermore, effective trial strategy does not require just any kind of jury research but jury research which is valid and reliable and conducted according to the canons of rigorous scientific method. Throughout this book, the terms research and pretrial research have occurred a good deal. It has been repeatedly emphasized that research and the way it is carried out is as important to the utilization of social science concepts as the concepts themselves. When an attorney is provided recommendations for trial strategy, the lawyer must have the confidence that he is getting what he is told he is getting. This confidence will be justified when there is reason to believe that the recommendations are based upon sound applications of methodology.

# Index

A

## C

## D



## E

## F



## H



## I



## J



## O

## S

## W





7941